Kid Trips Northern Virginia Edition: Your Family's Guide To Local Fun!

By Claudine Kurp, Amy Suski and Micaela Williamson

Preface

From historical sites and museums to nature centers, water parks, and children's theaters, Northern Virginia has an abundance of fun destinations and activities. Combined with its proximity to Washington, D.C., the Northern Virginia area is one of the best places in the country to raise a family.

Although this abundance can be overwhelming, ***Kid Trips Northern Virginia Edition*** puts these resources at your fingertips and provides useful **Insider Tips** for hundreds of local destinations and activities. And, because the fun doesn't stop at the shores of the Potomac River, don't miss our **Seasonal Guide** to annual events and family fun in D.C. and Maryland (including places that will hold the attention of your tween or teen). Additionally, if you're looking for the area's best services, check out our **Top Picks** for a special line-up of local family-friendly restaurants, great birthday party locations, shops, and much more.

We hope you enjoy your Kid Trips journey and make this a resource book that you continue to use again and again. But the fun doesn't have to stop here: stay connected by visiting us at www.GoKidTrips.com for the inside scoop on the latest local events and even more family fun!

One last note: although we did our best to provide the most current and accurate information available at the time of publication, this type of information is constantly changing. To avoid disappointment always check the venue's website or call ahead before heading out.

Dedication

This book is dedicated to our families. Without their love, patience, and enthusiastic participation, this book would not have been possible.

Table Of Contents

Chapter 1	Historical Sites and Museums	1
Chapter 2	Parks, Playgrounds, and Marinas	19
Chapter 3	Nature Centers	31
Chapter 4	Zoos, Farms, and Pick-Your-Own	43
Chapter 5	Playrooms, Bouncing, and Climbing	53
Chapter 6	Malls With Indoor Play Spaces	63
Chapter 7	Water Parks and Spraygrounds	67
Chapter 8	Ice Skating and Roller Skating	75
Chapter 9	Children's Theaters and Performances	83
Chapter 10	Miniature Golf	89
Chapter 11	Bowling	95
Chapter 12	Paintball Parks and Laser Tag	97
Chapter 13	Arts & Crafts	101
Chapter 14	Building Workshops	105
Chapter 15	Paint Your Own Pottery	109
Chapter 16	Jewelry Making	113
Chapter 17	Sports Teams and Venues	117
Chapter 18	Skateparks	123
Chapter 19	Campgrounds	127
Chapter 20	Amusement Parks	131

Chapter 21 Parent Support Groups **135**

Chapter 22 Childcare Support **141**

Chapter 23 Parenting Publications **143**

Chapter 24 Seasonal Fun **147**

Chapter 25 Family Fun Across the Potomac **179**

Chapter 26 Kid Trips Top Picks **195**

About The Authors **219**

Chapter 1

Historical Sites and Museums

Chapter 1: Historical Sites and Museums

Air Force Memorial
One Air Force Memorial Drive
Arlington, VA 22204
www.airforcememorial.org

Inspired by images of aircraft "soaring to victory", the Air Force Memorial opened in 2006 and is the site of many special events, including the free United States Air Force summertime concert series. Visit this impressive memorial near the Pentagon to honor and learn about the men and women who have served in the USAF. The memorial is walking distance from both the Pentagon Metro and the Pentagon City station metro (1/2 mile).

Alexandria Archaeology Museum
Torpedo Factory Art Center, 3rd Floor
105 North Union Street, Studio # 327
Alexandria, VA 22314
703-746-4399
www.alexandriava.gov/Archaeology

Connect with local archaeologists in this public laboratory and explore artifacts (some over 10,000 years old) by visiting exhibits, experiencing hands-on activities, or participating in a self-guided tour. Finds from current excavations are often on display. The staff is available to give guided tours to a minimum number of people with an advance reservation. While visiting the museum, explore the rest of the Torpedo Factory Arts Center, visit the waterfront, or take advantage of the fun shops and restaurants that Old Town Alexandria has to offer.

Alexandria Black History Museum
902 Wythe Street
Alexandria, Virginia 22314
703-746-4356
www.alexandriava.gov/BlackHistory

This museum displays local and regional history and also houses the Watson Reading Room. Exhibits concentrate on the history of slavery as well as how African-Americans helped shape and build past and present day communities. Right outside the museum is a nine-acre African American Heritage Park. A new component, the Contrabands and Freedman's Cemetery Memorial, is scheduled to open in 2013.

Arlington National Cemetery
Arlington, VA 22211
703-607-8000
www.arlingtoncemetery.mil

More than 330,000 American servicemen, servicewomen, and important Americans are buried at this famous 624-acre national cemetery. John F. Kennedy's gravesite is frequently visited and is home to the eternal flame. The Tomb of the Unknowns is guarded 24 hours a day and contains the remains of soldiers from WWI, WWII, Korea and Vietnam. Each hour (and each half-hour in the summer) there is an impressive changing of the guard ceremony. Approximately 30 new funerals are held here each day, so you will likely see multiple processions during your visit. Cars are allowed onto the grounds only by special permit, so be prepared to do a lot of walking. Bus tours allow visitors to hop on and off at the most popular sites. Pick up a tour guide, maps, books, and souvenirs in the Visitors' Center. Restroom facilities are also located in the Visitors' Center. The cemetery is Metro accessible by taking the Blue line to the Arlington National Cemetery stop.

Even though the cemetery is stroller-friendly, it may not be the best place to take toddlers, especially if they might have difficulty remaining quiet during the somber ceremonies. For older children, however, it is an important site not to be missed.

Insider Tip: If your children wonder how the eternal flame stays lit, tell them there is a gas burning system contained in a weather-proof box. According the Cemetery, it costs about $200 a month to keep the flame burning. Also, while you are there, be sure to visit Arlington House (a.k.a. the "Custis-Lee Mansion" and "The Robert E. Lee Memorial"), which was built by George Washington's family and lived in by Robert E. Lee and his wife until the Civil War. The house contains interesting information and artifacts and offers one of the best views of the Washington skyline. More information about visiting Arlington House can be found at www.nps.gov/arho.

Artisphere
1101 Wilson Boulevard
Arlington, VA 22209
703-875-1100
www.artisphere.com

The Artisphere is a visual arts museum and performance arts venue in one. Many art programs, workshops, movies and live shows are offered throughout the year, with kid-friendly programs too.

Ben Lomond Historic Site
10321 Sudley Manor Drive
Manassas, VA 20109
703-367-7872
www.pwcgov.org

Located within 5 miles of the first and second battle of Manassas, this historic property was occupied by both Confederate and Union soldiers. The property includes the main house and a 5,200 square foot garden that boasts one of the largest collections of roses out of the U.S. public gardens. Activities and events are scheduled regularly. Special programs are available for groups and scout troops.

Carlyle House
121 N. Fairfax Street
Alexandria, VA 22314
703-549-2997
www.nvrpa.org

Located in Old Town Alexandria across from City Hall, this historic property built in the 1750s offers tours, special events, and concerts. Programs that focus on children, like the "Hands on History Tent" series and "American Girl teas" frequent the site's event calendar. The Carlyle House is part of the Northern Virginia Regional Park system.

Insider Tip: Old Town Alexandria is a happening place to be! There is always something going on. Explore fun modes of transportation such as the free King Street trolley, take a boat tour or embark on a pirate cruise. For more information about Old Town Alexandria and the free King Street trolleys, visit www.visitalexandriava.com. Information about boat tours is available at the Potomac Riverboat Company site: www.potomacriverboatco.com.

Cherry Hill Farmhouse
312 Park Avenue
Falls Church, VA 22046
703-248-5171
www.cherryhillfallschurch.org

This historic farmhouse displays life as it was for a middle class family living in mid-19th century Virginia. House tours by costumed attendants, scout programs, and special activities such as "Victoria Tea and Manners for Children," happen throughout the year. The house is sometimes rented out for private events, so please check the website or call ahead before visiting.

Insider Tip: The Cherry Hill Farmhouse is adjacent to Cherry Hill Park, a wonderful children's playground with picnic facilities and easy access to restrooms in the City of Falls Church Community Center (on the same grounds) or in the Mary Stiles Library across the street.

Colvin Run Mill
10017 Colvin Run Road
Great Falls, VA 22066
703-759-2771
www.fairfaxcounty.gov/parks/crm

Colvin Run Mill is a restored water-powered mill built in 1811 that still grinds cornmeal, wheat flour, and grits. Visit the historic site and hear the story of the family that ran the mill for more than fifty years. Personalized tours by a friendly and knowledgeable staff are available. Explore the beautiful grounds and hiking trails. Be sure and also visit the general store to buy flour from the mill, "penny" candy, toys, books, and other mementos. Special programs such as concerts, ice cream making, and craft fairs are held throughout the year.

DEA Museum (Drug Enforcement Administration Museum)
700 Army Navy Drive
Arlington, VA 22202
202-307-3463
www.deamuseum.org

Permanent multimedia exhibits here include "Illegal Drugs in America: a Modern History" and "Good Medicine, Bad Behavior." Traveling exhibits circle through. Admission is free, and there is also a gift shop stocked with an extensive supply of merchandise, clothing, and accessories that carry the official DEA seal. The DEA Museum is located across from the Pentagon City Mall and is metro accessible. Best suited for older children.

Fairfax Station Railroad Museum
11200 Fairfax Station Road
Fairfax Station, VA 22039
703-425-9225
www.fairfax-station.org

A former train depot from Civil War times, this museum is now a place to learn about community history, the Civil War and, of course, see model trains. The museum is small and is usually only open on Sundays from 1-4 p.m. Kids will enjoy the intricate model train displays and climbing in the old caboose located on the museum grounds. Special events and tours are held throughout the year.

Fort Ward Museum and Historic Site
4301 West Braddock Road
Alexandria, VA 22304
703-838-4340
www.alexandriava.gov/FortWard

Fort Ward Museum features Civil War exhibits, artifacts, tours and living history programs. Walk the 40+ acre Fort Ward Park to see cannons, bombproofs, and reconstructed quarters of civil war soldiers. Special events, concerts, and war re-enactments held throughout the year.

Insider Tip: Every summer, 8-12 year-olds can participate in a Civil War Kids' Camp, which includes games, Civil War-era food, camping lessons, and visits by re-enactors.

Freeman Store and Museum
131 Church Street NE
Vienna, VA 22180
703-938-5187
www.historicviennainc.org

The Freeman Store sells distinctive Virginia gifts and products, candy, and old-fashioned toys. The upstairs museum has rotating exhibits and is open to the public. Special events, such as free holiday visits with Santa, occur periodically.

Friendship Firehouse Museum
107 S. Alfred Street
Alexandria, VA 22314
703-746-3891
www.alexandriava.gov/FriendshipFirehouse

Learn about the history of volunteer fire companies in Alexandria and view antique carriages, fire tools, and gear. The museum is located in Old Town Alexandria near lots of shops, restaurants, and attractions. The museum is small, so plan to spend only 30-40 minutes at most, but nonetheless, it is a fun venue for firehouse fans.

Gadsby's Tavern Museum
134 N. Royal Street
Alexandria, VA 22314
703-746-4242
www.alexandriava.gov/GadsbysTavern

Gadsby's Tavern has been around since 1785 with notable patrons including George Washington, John Adams, Thomas Jefferson, James Madison, James Monroe, and the Marquis de Lafayette. The museum is only open to scheduled tours. Educational programs for community students and scouts are available, as well as "Tavern in a Trunk" programs in which the museum staff brings artifacts and primary resource documents directly to students. Special events, teas, and family days are held throughout the year.

Insider Tip: Families with toddlers can participate in Tavern Toddlers, a popular weekly drop-in open play session in the museum from September-April. See the programs and events section on the website for details.

George Washington Masonic Memorial
101 Callahan Drive
Alexandria, VA 22301
703-683-2007
www.gwmemorial.org/

Standing tall in the sky at the entrance to Old Town Alexandria, it is hard to miss this memorial. The three-tier tower has six floors open for tours with public exhibits about the Masonic Fraternity, but kids will just enjoy the views and running up the huge stairs "Rocky" style. Pair a visit to this site with a trip to Old Town where you can enjoy the shops and restaurants, or take a free trolley ride up and down King Street.

Greater Reston Arts Center
12001 Market Street
Reston, VA 20190
703-471-9242
www.restonarts.org

An actual art museum that is kid-friendly! Preschool and elementary aged children will love dropping in this art center during gallery hours and getting a bucket full of art supplies to tote around. This "Explore More" program gives families a guide to encourage conversation and creativity while visiting the exhibits. Other special family-friendly events are scheduled regularly.

Insider Tip: This museum is located in Reston Town Center, a fun downtown area with lots of shops, restaurants, frequent free entertainment, and even a play fountain for little ones in the summer months. See www.restontowncenter.com for a calendar of events and directory.

Gunston Hall
10709 Gunston Road
Lorton, VA 22079
703-550-9220
www.gunstonhall.org

Former home of George Mason, author the Virginia Declaration of Rights, the property includes a mansion, museum, and historic grounds. The visit begins with an 11-minute film about George Mason and house tours are offered every half hour. Although there are family-friendly events offered throughout the year, Gunston Hall is best for older children who can understand more about colonial history.

Insider Tip: The March Kite Festival is considered to be one of the area's best family events. Your children will be amazed at the magical and artistic kites soaring overhead. Another fun special event, Plantation Christmas, includes horse drawn carriage rides, apple cider, treats, and costumed characters.

Haymarket Museum
15025 Washington Street
Haymarket, VA 20169
703-753-3712
www.haymarketmuseum.org

The Haymarket Museum is located in an old church and schoolhouse, but is actually a part of a small museum system in the historical town of Haymarket. Besides the museum, there are a few historic homes, an old post office and St. Paul's Church. The museum is part of Virginia's Civil War trails.

Iwo Jima Memorial (United States Marine Corps Memorial)
1400 N. Meade Street
Arlington, VA 22209
703- 289-2500
www.nps.gov

Dedicated to Marines who have given their lives for the United States since 1775, this iconic memorial is breathtaking to visit. Tuesday evenings during the summer, the Marines host Sunset Parades at the Memorial.

During the one hour performance, the U.S. Marine Drum and Bugle Corps present music and showcase precision drills. The Sunset Parade is open to the public at no charge. Visitors are welcome to bring lawn chairs, blankets, strollers, and picnics. Drivers beware: driving access and parking is closed off starting several hours before each parade. Parking with shuttle bus service is available at Arlington National Cemetery for a small fee. The memorial is also about a 10-minute walk from the Rosslyn Metro station. There are portable toilets at the memorial but no food facilities.

Lee-Fendall House Museum and Gardens
614 Oronoco Street
Alexandria, VA 22314
703-548-1789
www.leefendallhouse.org

At various times in its history, this 18th century white clapboard home in Old Town Alexandria was home to the Revolutionary War Hero Henry "Light Horse Harry" Lee, his son Confederate General Robert E. Lee, housed hundreds of convalescing Union soldiers during the Civil War, was home to the prominent Downham family, and home to one of the nations most controversial labor leaders, John L. Lewis. Today it has been restored to its early Victorian elegance during the period when the Lee family lived there. The house is furnished with a collection of Lee family heirlooms, period furniture, portraits, and silver. You may visit the garden without a ticket, but to see the house you will have to purchase a ticket for a guided tour. Children under 5 are free.

Insider Tip: The Lee-Fendall House Easter Egg Hunt event is very popular, so make reservations early, beginning February 1. Special teas and Victorian etiquette programs are also available for Girl Scouts.

Loudoun Museum
16 Loudoun Street SW
Leesburg, VA 20175
703-777-7427
www.loudounmuseum.org

History comes alive for families with exhibits filled with artifacts from the past such as household items, war relics, tools, and clothing. There is a Discovery Room for children and tours, lectures, and programs are offered on a regular basis. The museum is located in Historic Downtown Leesburg, which is filled with history, unique shops, and restaurants.

Loudoun Heritage Farm Museum
21668 Heritage Farm Lane
Sterling, VA 20164
571-258-3800
www.heritagefarmmuseum.org

Located on the grounds of Claude Moore Park, the Heritage Farm Museum has artifacts from the agricultural past and hands-on-play areas for children. Although there are learning exhibits for older children, the museum is best enjoyed by children ages 0 - 6. Young ones will love playing in the old-fashioned farm kitchen, working at the general store, milking a cow, pedaling a tractor, and doing other imaginary farm chores. The staff frequently runs special programs for scouts and annual events such as Tractorpooloza, Bunny Bonanza, and the Princess for a Day Ice Cream Social are popular community favorites.

Insider Tip: The museum also hosts various "parents night out" opportunities throughout the year, and is a great venue for preschoolers to have birthday parties.

The Lyceum
201 S. Washington Street
Alexandria, VA 22314
703-746-4994
www.alexandriava.gov/Lyceum

Head to the Lyceum in Old Town Alexandria to learn all about the rich history of the City of Alexandria. Special programs, performances, and lectures are offered throughout the year. The Lyceum Museum shop contains maps, books, cards, and mementos of Alexandria's history.

Manassas National Battlefield
6511 Sudley Road
Manassas, VA 20109
703-361-1339
www.nps.gov/mana

Part of the National Park service, this Civil War battleground has a visitor center with museum, monuments, bookstore, wooded hiking trails, and a huge meadow. There are driving tours and directions to access a number of important historical sites, but children will likely be most interested in the Henry Hill Visitor Center and exploring the grounds around the center. The museum has Civil War era weapons and uniforms, a 45-minute orientation film, and a few interactive displays.

With or without a visit to the museum, the 5,200-acre site is well worth the visit with scenic views and outdoor activities such as hiking, catch and release fishing, and horseback riding (BYOH= bring your own horse.) The park is also a popular place for picnics and family photos.

Insider Tip: The battlefield contains a variety of ticks, so be sure to take precautions when walking through the long grass and wooded areas. Pets are allowed on leashes. Picnics are allowed in designated areas.

Manassas Museum
9101 Prince William Street
Manassas, VA 20110
703-368-1873
www.manassasmuseum.org

This 7,000 square-foot museum houses many permanent and temporary exhibits, videos, artifacts, and documents that exhibit Northern Virginia history. Traveling trunks are available for check out for students in grades 1-6, complete with teachers' guides and hands-on materials. Little kids will love "Toddler Tuesday" programs, held on select Tuesdays of the month.

Insider Tip: Echoes, the museum store, boasts an impressive collection of original prints and collectibles as well as many toys, books, jewelry, and household items. It is a great place to find a unique gift for history lovers young and old.

Mary Washington House
1200 Charles Street
Fredericksburg, VA 22401
540-373-1569
www.preservationvirginia.org

Tour the farmhouse George Washington bought for his mother Mary and relish in the beauty of the gardens. Here you can learn a little bit about 18th century life and the history of the Washington family. Family-friendly programs with refreshments happen the first Saturday of each month. The museum is located in the city of Fredericksburg near the historic downtown district.

Mount Vernon Estate & Gardens
George Washington Parkway
Alexandria, VA 22121
703-780-2000
www.mountvernon.org

Former home of George Washington, the 500-acre working farm and estate features an expansive new museum, theatre and visitors center, but your kids may be happiest roaming the pastoral riverfront grounds and visiting the farm animals. However much fun you are having, be sure to stop for a reverent moment at Washington's tomb. Tours of the beautifully restored historic mansion feature original objects from 1740s and are best appreciated by older children. During peak season the lines for house tours can be extremely long. For an added fee boat rides on the Potomac River are available. Visit for the day or buy an annual pass to enjoy the 500-acre estate and special events year-round. Mount Vernon is open 365 days a year.

Insider Tip: For a special meal, try the Mount Vernon Inn Restaurant, located right on the grounds and serving regional and colonial cuisine. Reservations are recommended and can be made by calling 703-780-0011. Need something quick? There is also a large food court with snacks, sandwiches, soups, and pizza options.

Morven Park and the Winmill Carriage Collection
17263 Southern Planter Lane
Leesburg, VA 20176
703-777-6034
www.morvenpark.org

With over 1,000-acres of lawns, woods, and gardens, this beautiful setting is the home to many equestrian events and special programs. Guided tours of the Movern Park mansion are offered, but kids will most likely enjoy the Winmill Carriage Collection. With over 120 carriages on display from the mid 1800s and early 1900s, children will marvel at the antique modes of transportation. One popular carriage is the miniature Road Coach once owned by "General Tom Thumb" of the Barnum and Bailey Circus.

Insider Tip: While in Leesburg, visit the fun downtown area. Check out the shops, restaurants, and visit the events calendar at www.leesburgva.gov. Do you love to shop? The Leesburg Corner Premium Outlets, www.premiumoutlets.com, offer great deals on upscale merchandise.

National Air & Space Museum Udvar-Hazy Center
14390 Air and Space Museum Parkway
Chantilly, VA 20151
www.airandspace.si.edu/udvarhazy

Located a short distance from Dulles International Airport, the Udvar-Hazy Center displays such grand dames as the B-29 Superfortress Enola Gay, Concorde, Lockheed Martin SR-71 Blackbird, Boeing Stratoliner, and most recently, the Space Shuttle Discovery. Udvar-Hazy was created to house those special treasures that are too large for the Air & Space Museum in Washington, DC. Together the two sites house the largest collection of aviation and space artifacts in the world. Admission is free, but public parking is $15 (free parking daily after 4 p.m.)

Be sure to take the elevator up to the Observation Tower for a great view of planes taking off and landing at Dulles Airport. The museum also contains an IMAX theater and flight simulator rides (for a fee). Food options include McDonald's, McCafe, or packaged snacks in the gift shop like "astronaut ice cream." (For more dining options, drive over to the nearby Reston Town Center after your visit.) The gift shop is popular with kids and has a large selection of model airplanes, toys, apparel, and aviation books.

Insider Tip: Super Science Saturdays are offered the second Saturday of the month. This popular educational program for kids can get crowded, so try to arrive early.

National Firearms Museum
11250 Waples Mill Road
Fairfax, VA 22030
703-267-1600
www.nramuseum.org

Even for someone who cringes at a child's use of a water pistol, this museum was fascinating. With over 15 galleries focused on different historical periods and important figures, there is a lot to see and learn here. President Theodore Roosevelt's collection of guns, gear, and safari treasures is especially interesting. While this wouldn't be a great choice for a grade school outing, tween and teens should be able to appreciate the history that can be learned here. Located in the headquarters of the National Rifle Association, the museum's galleries include exhibits on New World explorers, the Revolutionary War, the exploration of the American West, the Civil War, military guns, guns belonging to royal families, Hollywood guns, toy guns and more. NRA Headquarters also has a cafe and gift store open to the public. Parking is free.

National Inventors Hall of Fame and Museum
600 Dulany Street
Alexandria, VA 22314
www.uspto.gov/about/offices/opa/museum.jsp

Located in the atrium of the United States Patent and Trademark Offices in Alexandria, this new venue features interactive exhibits, a high definition video theatre, portrait gallery, and a gift shop. Through the magic of computer-generated special effects, portraits of famous inventors such as Thomas Jefferson, Thomas Edison, and Steve Wozniak, the co-founder of Apple Computer, come to life and talk about the history of invention. Visitors will also learn about the protections of intellectual property rights through patents, trademarks, copyrights, and trade secrets such as the formula for Coca-Cola. The museum is open weekdays only and is free. Although area parking is tight, the museum is accessible from the King Street and Eisenhower Avenue Metro stations.

National Museum of the Marine Corps
18900 Jefferson Davis Highway
Triangle, VA 22134
800-397-7585
www.usmcmuseum.org

A tribute to the United States Marine Corps, past, present, and future, this museum boasts state-of-the-art exhibits filled with artifacts, historical replications, and interactive experiences. Since the purpose is to show the history of the Marine Corps, many displays include battle scenes with casualties. This may be disturbing for young children, so please use your best judgment or call ahead with any questions. Signs are posted at some exhibits warning that they may not be kid-friendly. A free copy of the "Young Visitor's Gallery Hunt," recommended for ages 4-10 is available at the front desk and on the website.

For a small fee, visitors of all ages can visit the rifle range and shoot laser beams from a gun with the same weight and feel as a real one. Popular family days are held the second Saturday of each month, which may include puppet shows, crafts, movies, and interactive activities.

Insider Tip: Upstairs from the galleries, the Mess Hall and Tun Tavern provide meals and snacks inside the museum. The Tun Tavern is a particularly charming reproduction of the colonial tavern in Philadelphia considered to be the birthplace of the Corps. Although the tavern fare is surprisingly good, the dining experience is considerably longer than that of the Mess Hall -- something to consider if time is a factor or you have restless little ones.

Old Town Alexandria Tours & Scavenger Hunts
www.visitalexandriava.com
www.alexcolonialtours.com
www.christmasattic.com

Adventurous families will love the Ghost & Graveyard Tour, Historic Walking Tour, African-American History Tour, and Scavenger Hunts along the brick-lined streets of Old Town Alexandria. To get started, call ahead to book a private tour guide with Alexandria Colonial Tours, download one of the free self-guided walking tours posted on VisitAlexandriaVA.com, or purchase an inexpensive Scavenger Hunt map at the Christmas Attic at 125 S. Union Street. Either way, the family will learn plenty of fun facts about George Washington and Old Town Alexandria. Finish off the day with a wonderful lunch at one of the many restaurants such as the Union Street Public House that line the historic streets of Old Town.

Oatlands Plantation
20850 Oatlands Plantation Lane
Leesburg, VA 20175
703-777-3174
www.oatlands.org

Located on scenic grounds outside the town of Leesburg, this historic property includes a mansion and beautiful gardens. A visit to the property, which includes a house tour, is best for older children. However, there are seasonal family programs, such as festivals and outdoor theater performances for younger children. Afternoon tea experiences, such as the Teddy Bear Tea, are offered throughout the year and require advance reservations.

Insider Tip: See tips from Morven Park and the Winmill Carriage Collection regarding visiting the surrounding area of Leesburg.

The Pentagon
1400 Defense Pentagon
Washington, DC 20301
703-697-1776
http://pentagontours.osd.mil/

In spite of its official address, this iconic military headquarters is actually located in Arlington, Virginia. It is possible to tour the Pentagon, but reservations must be made well in advance and tours book up quickly. Please visit the website to view the tour guidelines and security information before requesting a tour. Tours last about 60 minutes and include around 1.5 miles of walking. The tours focus on the mission of the Department of Defense, momentous moments in military history, and include a visit to the 9/11 Memorial. Public parking is no longer available at the Pentagon. Visitors may want to park at Pentagon City Mall and walk 5 minutes through pedestrian tunnels. The mall and its surrounding area (Pentagon Row) are also good options for meals or snacks. Tours are not recommended for young children.

Reston Museum
1639 Washington Plaza North
Reston, VA 20190
703-709-7700
www.restonmuseum.org

Focusing on the town of Reston, this museum has rotating exhibits, special events, and regular family programs. The museum is located in Lake Anne Plaza, which is home to shops, restaurants and regular outdoor entertainment. For added seasonal fun, families can rent a paddle boat .

Rippon Lodge
15520 Blackburn Road
Woodbridge VA 22191
703-499-9812
www.pwcgov.org

Part of the National Underground Railroad Network to Freedom and National Wildlife Federation, Rippon Lodge consists of a historic house, formal gardens, cemetery, and 43-acres of walking trails. Tours of Rippon Lodge are offered May-October, and family events, nature walks, and history programs take place throughout the year.

River Farm
7931 East Boulevard Drive
Alexandria VA 22308
703-768-5700
www.ahs.org/river_farm

River Farm serves as the headquarters for the American Horticultural Society (AHS) and is open to the public with free admission. The Andre Bluemel Meadow is breathtaking with more than 100,000 plants. The children's garden is designed for kids to explore and play and regular children's programs are scheduled for budding gardeners, as well as special programs for scouts, school groups, and homeschoolers.

Sully Historic Site
3650 Historic Sully Way
Chantilly, VA 20151
703-437-1794
www.fairfaxcounty.gov/parks/sully/

Sully Historic Site includes a museum, historical house, outbuildings, representative slave quarters, and gardens. The home was completed in 1799 by Richard Bland Lee, uncle of Confederate General Robert E. Lee, and is one of the finest examples of Georgian and Federal architecture in Northern Virginia. Interactive videos, exhibits, hands-on activities for children, and hourly guided tours highlight the early 19th century life of the Lee family, tenant farmers and enslaved African Americans. The property is part of the Fairfax County Parks system and special family programs, festivals, and events happen throughout the year. In the summer time, come for one of the "Dairy Days" to churn butter, crank ice cream, and play old-fashioned games.

United States Geological Survey
USGS National Center
12201 Sunrise Valley Drive
Reston, VA 20192
703-648-5953
www.usgs.gov

On a visit to the Nation's leading earth and biological science agency, children can participate in hands-on science activities and learn through guided tours or special programs. Please note that guided tours are suggested and are only available through reservation. Self-guided tours are available without a reservation during designated hours.

If the weather permits, be sure to visit the Woodland Walk and Rock Garden Walk. Suggested for ages 8 and older.

Weem-Botts Museum
3944 Cameron Street
Dumfries, VA 22026
703-221-2218
www.historicdumfries.com

This small museum shows the history of the town of Dumfries, Virginia's oldest chartered town. The tour is interesting for older children and teens and mentions that the house is actively haunted today. Special family events are held throughout the year.

Woodlawn Plantation & Pope-Leighey House
9000 Richmond Highway
Mount Vernon, VA 22309
703-780-4000
www.woodlawn1805.org
www.popeleighey1940.org
www.arcadiafood.org

Adjacent to Mount Vernon, the grounds of Woodlawn Plantation are home to the beautiful Georgian style home of Washington's nephew and the Pope-Leighey house, one of Frank Lloyd Wright's most famously designed homes, and the Arcadia Center for Sustainable Food and Agriculture. It is possible to walk from Mount Vernon to Woodlawn, but with children it's easier to drive. Guided tours of both houses are available. Visitors are welcome to view the sustainable food practices at Arcadia. High tea is served at the Woodlawn Plantation and special farm-to-table dinners are served at Arcadia by reservation. Woodlawn Plantation is closed January and February, except for President's Day.

Chapter 2

Parks, Playgrounds, and Marinas

Chapter 2: Parks, Playgrounds & Marinas

Algonkian Park and Bull Run Marina
47001 Fairway Drive
Sterling, VA 20165
703.450.4655
www.nvrpa.org/park/algonkian

If you are looking for a perfect day of family fun or a great destination for a "staycation" you have found it. Algonkian Park boasts the crazy fun Volcano Island Waterpark, miniature golf, fun trails for older children, picnic shelters and a boat launch with access to the Bull Run Marina. The waterpark is perfect for children of all ages. For those that might decide to stay a bit longer, riverfront cottage rentals are available. Algonkian Park rests on the banks of the Potomac River and is open year round. The waterpark is open seasonally. The trails around the park and the Potomac River are not stroller friendly. Guided nature hikes and walks are also offered. The park also hosts the popular NVRPA Roving Naturalist Program. Restrooms are available throughout the park. Admission to the park is free, however, some activities and rentals may require a fee. Check the website for the most up to date rate schedule.

Barcroft Park
4200 S. Four Mile Run Drive
Arlington, VA 22206
www.co.arlington.va.us

Located on 65-acres in the heart of Arlington, Barcroft Park is a year-round urban oasis of fun and activities. The park offers a playground for school age and pre-school children. The park is also a perfect venue for a family picnic. There are picnic shelters, tables, charcoal grills and a horseshoe pit. Restrooms are available. Paved trails are best with a buddy. Always be mindful of safety when using the trails. If you are heading to the park with older kids you can also enjoy biking, hiking and nature trails with streams.

Bull Run Regional Park
7700 Bull Run Drive
Centreville, VA 20121
703-631-0550
http://www.nvrpa.org/park/bull_run

See Chapter 3: Nature Centers

Burke Lake Park, Golf Course and Marina
7315 Ox Road
Fairfax, VA 22039
703-323-6600
www.fairfaxcounty.gov/parks/burkelake

Burke Lake Park has long been a local favorite for those in Northern Virginia. The main attraction for many is the 218-acre lake that offers visitors fishing, boating, and rowboat rentals. Boat rentals can be a wonderful way to explore the idyllic setting from a unique view.

Burke Lake Park also gets an A+ for ease. Many of the family friendly amenities are steps from the parking lot. The main area for small children is stroller friendly. If you are visiting the park with young children be sure to take advantage of the quaint miniature train that takes you on a magical ride around the park. Children will also enjoy a carousel, clubhouse with ice cream parlor and playground. Restrooms are also available both in the ice cream parlor and near the marina.

Walking trails abound but many require a sturdy stroller. While the water can be very alluring, swimming is prohibited. Admission is free for Fairfax County residents. Fees apply for non-resident admission, miniature golf, the carousel, the train and the boat rentals.

Insider Tip: There are a few mommy friendly jogging groups that meet at Burke Lake Park. Visit www.seemommyrun.com/va for more information.

Claude Moore Park
21544 Old Vestal's Gap Road
Sterling, VA 20164
571-258-3700
www.loudoun.gov

See Chapter 4: Zoos, Farms, and Pick-Your-Own

Chessie's Big Backyard @ Lee District Park
6601 Telegraph Road
Alexandria, Virginia 22310
703-922-9840
www.fairfaxparkfoundation.org

A beautiful woodland theme playground, Chessie's Big Backyard offers slides, accessible ramps, tunnels, steering wheels, rock climbing structures and more. Please note that this playground is in direct sunlight, but shade is available in a large picnic pavilion and the giant wooded deck trail named "the Treehouse."

Bathroom facilities are only open from the spring to early fall. The playground is located next to the sprayground.

Clemyjontri Park
6317 Georgetown Pike
McLean, VA 22101
703-388-2807
www.fairfaxcounty.gov/parks/clemyjontri

This two-acre kiddie wonderland has an incredible offering of climbing structures, swings, mazes, seesaws, a mini-rock climbing wall, oodles of slides and a charming carousel.

The park was designed to be accessible to children with all abilities. Rubber surfaces, wide opening to play structures and lower monkey bars are just some of the features that allow for unique and inclusive playground experience. The park is wheelchair accessible and has restrooms and vending machines. There is also a picnic pavilion that can be used by the public and rented for birthday parties. As newly planted trees have not yet filled out to provide shade, be sure to bring sun protection on sunny days. The park is free to enter but there is a small fee to ride the carousel. Seasonal hours apply for the carousel.

Insider Tip: The secret is out. Many locals have discovered this innovative and inviting park. While there are ample handicap spots in the parking lot, there is often a shortage of regular spots on busy days. Plan on bringing a stroller, as you may need to walk from the lot across the street. The trek is worth it, however.

Fort Hunt Park
George Washington Pkwy 6 miles south of Old Town
899 Fort Hunt Road
Alexandria, VA 22308
202-439-7325
www.nps.gov/gwmp/planyourvisit/forthunt.htm

Fort Hunt Park has a storied past. Once owned by George Washington, the park sits near the edge of the Potomac River on the Virginia side. Fort Hunt was defended during the Spanish American War and operated as a center for intelligence and document reviews during WWII. Thankfully, the park is much quieter these days.

Visitors can take advantage of trails that can accommodate walkers and bicyclists. Strollers can be used on the paved loop road. Picnic pavilions are available but must be reserved from April to October. Fort Hunt Park is open year-round and closes at sunset. A small playground, public restrooms and parking lots are available.

Fountainhead Regional Park (On-site Marina)
10875 Hampton Road
Fairfax Station, VA 22039
703-250-9124
www.nvrpa.org/park/fountainhead

Sitting on the banks of the Occoquan River, Fountainhead Regional Park offers a paradise for boating enthusiasts. Kayak, canoe, and 3 to 4 person boat rentals are available for visitors. They even offer kayak tours! The park also offers a miniature golf, a snack shop, hiking trails and mountain biking. There are stroller friendly paths that are located in the park. Restrooms are available. The park is open from dawn until dusk but has varied seasonal hours. Check the website for the most up to date hours before making your trip.

Great Falls Park
9200 Old Dominion Drive
McLean, VA 22102
703-285-2965
www.nps.gov/grfa

Great Falls is truly a majestic sight to behold. Perched on the edge of the Potomac River, the view from Mather Gorge's cliff tops is captivating. Although there are interesting historic markers and wildlife to be seen throughout the 800-acre park, the highlights of the park are Overlooks 1, 2 & 3, accessible by short trails from the nature center. For those with little ones, Overlook 2 and Overlook 3 are stroller friendly and handicap accessible. Although barriers exist between onlookers and the steep Overlook drops, always carefully watch young children and be aware of safety whenever you are hiking close to the river. Due to the dangerous rapids, swimming and wading are strictly prohibited.

Take advantage of the park's Junior Ranger Program for children ages 5 and up. A booklet and two hours is all you need to have your child earn a Junior Ranger badge. Picnic tables and grills are available on a first come, first serve basis. There is a small fee to enter the park. Guided tours are available and a "Schedule of Events" is listed on the website. The park is open daily from 7 a.m. until dark. A visitor center, parking lots and restrooms are available. Dogs and pets are welcome but must be kept on a 6-foot leash.

Ida Lee Park Recreation Center
25 West Market Street
Leesburg, VA 20178
703-777-2420
www.idalee.org

The pride of the Leesburg Parks and Recreation Department, Ida Lee Park features an impressive family friendly recreation center. A fitness center, indoor and outdoor swimming, a larger tennis complex and impressive line-up of recreational programs are offered to the public. Ida Lee Recreation Center also offers a Kids Corner childcare center. Fees apply for the fitness center, childcare and classes. Check the website for the most update information on fees and hours. Apart from the recreation center, visitors can enjoy 2 outdoor playgrounds, a picnic shelter and cross country trails free of charge. The trails are not stroller friendly.

Jefferson Falls District Park
7900 Lee Highway
Falls Church, VA 22042
703-573-0444
www.fairfaxcounty.gov/parks/golf/jeffersongc

The park offers miniature golf, a playground, lit tennis courts, basketball courts and a picnic area. Refreshments and restrooms are available. Fees apply for miniature golf. The park is open year round from dawn to sundown. The site is stroller friendly.

Lake Accotink Park and Marina
7500 Accotink Park Road
Springfield, VA 22150
703-569-0285
www.fairfaxcounty.gov/parks/accotink

Located in Springfield, just off of I-495, Lake Accotink Park is a hidden gem nestled in Fairfax County. The 493-acre park includes a huge 55-acre lake. Families flock to the park for the antique carousel, picnic pavilions with grills, playgrounds, volleyball and tennis courts and miniature golf. The picturesque marina offers paddle, canoe and rowboat rentals. In addition to the host of kid friendly amenities, the park also has a snack bar, walking trails and public restrooms. The park is open daily year-round from 7 a.m. until dusk. Some pavilion areas may require a reservation. The common areas are stroller friendly.

Insider Tip: Nature lovers will enjoy the endless wetlands and views of marsh life. Trails require a sturdy stroller to navigate.

Lake Ridge Park and Marina
12350 Cotton Mill Drive
Woodbridge, Virginia 22192
703 494-5464
www.pwcparks.org

Located in Prince William County on the Occoquan Reservoir, Lake Ridge Park offers a marina with kayak, canoe, rowboat and paddleboat rentals. There is a playground, picnic pavilion, hiking trails, and a miniature golf course that is open seasonally. In addition, Lake Ridge Park offers student science programs. The marina, playground area and most trails are stroller friendly. Restrooms are available in the activity center located near the marina. Fees apply to boat rentals and miniature golf. The park is open from sunrise to dusk year-round. Hours and offerings change seasonally. Call ahead to confirm operating hours.

Leesylvania State Park and Marina
2001 Daniel K. Ludwig Drive
Woodbridge, VA 22129
703-730-8205
www.dcr.virginia.gov/state_parks/lee.shtml

This 542-acre park in Prince William County borders the Potomac River and holds historical significance as the birthplace of Revolutionary War hero "Light Horse" Harry Lee, the father of Confederate General Robert E. Lee. The park's visitor center features historical displays of the park's rich history. The center also has a discovery area that features live turtles and nature displays.

The park offers nature and historical walks, educational classes, canoe tours, hiking trails and fishing. Sailboat rentals are offered through a private on-site company. The marina has a concession stand that serves burgers, hot dogs and beverages. The park also has a playground and picnic area. Seasonally there is a "Music at the Marina" concert series. Restrooms are available throughout the park. Many of the common areas and some trails are stroller friendly. The park is open year-round from 6 a.m. to sunset. Admission fees apply.

Insider Tip: The park has a rich calendar of events that include an annual Civil War reenactment that takes place in late September on or near the Anniversary of the Potomac River Blockade. Expect to see cannons and muskets. Sign up for the park's newsletter to see all of the latest happenings.

Locust Shade Park and Marina
4701 Locust Shade Drive
Triangle, VA 22172
703 221-8579
www.pwcgov.org

Locust Shade Park is another Prince William County hidden gem. This 400-acre haven of outdoor fun has something for the whole family. Visitors are treated to miniature golf, batting cages, a driving range, tennis courts, hiking trails and plenty of fishing. The park also offers a playground, a picnic area, barbecue grills and a sand volleyball court. The marina rests on an eight-acre lake and offers pedal boat rentals on the weekends from May until September. For fishing enthusiasts, the pond is stocked regularly with trout and catfish seasonally. Fishing can only be done from the bank during park hours.

Restrooms are available. The park is stroller friendly and even has a steady stream of mommy groups that walk the park in the mornings. Entrance to the park is free. Fees apply to park activities. The park is open from 8 a.m. until 8 p.m. Activity availability is seasonal. Many of the activities are closed by November. Call ahead to confirm hour of operation.

Insider Tip: Locust Shade Park shines in the summer months with an evening concert series held in a 500-seat amphitheater. Sign up for the Locust Shade Park newsletter to stay connected.

Manassas National Battlefield
6511 Sudley Road
Manassas, VA 20109
(703) 361-1339
www.nps.gov/mana

See Chapter 1: Historical Sites and Museums

Occoquan Bay National Wildlife Refuge
13950 Dawson Beach Road
Woodbridge, VA 22191
703-490-4979
www.fws.gov/refuges

See Chapter 3: Nature Centers

Pohick Bay Regional Park and Marina
Pirates Cove Waterpark
6501 Pohick Bay Drive
Lorton, VA 22079
703-339-6104
www.nvrpa.org/park/pohick_bay
www.piratescovepohick.com

Located on the Potomac River in Fairfax County and 25 miles from Washington DC, Pohick Bay Regional Park offers an array of fun activities for the water enthusiasts and those seeking family fun. Kayaks, canoes and paddleboats are available for rental in the marina area. If you are taking smaller children, the main activity hubs are all stroller friendly. Pohick Bay Regional Park offers a miniature golf, a large playground, picnic areas and hiking trails for older children.

During the summer visitors can enjoy the Pirates Cove Waterpark. Kids will enjoy a 300-gallon dumping bucket and the Buccaneer Beach sand play area. Pirate's Cove has a snack bar, a picnic area and a sunning deck. Birthday parties and swim lessons are also offered. Restrooms are available in the park and inside Pirate's Cove Waterpark. The park is open year-round from sunrise to sunset. Admission to the park is free, but many of the water activities require a fee. Pirate's Cove is opened seasonally. Check the website for the up to date fee schedule.

Potomac Overlook Regional Park
2845 N. Marcey Road
Arlington, VA
703-528-5406
www.nvrpa.org/park/potomac_overlook

See Chapter 3: Nature Centers

Powhatan Springs Park
6020 Wilson Boulevard
Arlington, VA 22205
703-228-PLAY
www.arlingtonva.us

This unique Arlington park features a 15, 000 square foot skatepark, children's rain garden and a youth athletic field for soccer and lacrosse. The skatepark has a combination of street-style elements for skateboarding and in-line skating. Helmets are required. Children under the age of 10 must be accompanied by an adult in the skatepark. The rain garden is a wonderful place for young children to learn about the collection and conservation of water through interactive fun with water. Children can hop from stone to stone and see wetland plants, play in drops of water, watch water being collected and pumped, and place objects in a flume and watch them float downstream.

Prince William Forest Park
State Route 619 West
Triangle, VA 22122
703-221-7181
www.nps.gov/prwi

Run by the National Park Service and located near Manassas National Battlefield Park, Prince William Park has 37 miles of hiking trails to explore. Little ones can enjoy a large playground, picnic area and a few shorter trails with educational signage. Older children can take advantage of longer, day-long hikes. There is a fun series of ranger-led programs for children of all ages that help children discover the beauty and nature of the park. With 4 campgrounds, 100 cabins, and summertime Saturday night campfire programs, Prince William Park is an ideal venue for a family camping trip. There are entrance and camping fees. There is a visitor center with restrooms. The park is open year-round from 9 a.m. to 5 p.m. daily. The visitor center is closed on some major holidays.

Insider Tip: You don't need to conquer the park by tackling the miles of trails on foot. There is a 12-mile scenic drive that allows you explore the park by car. Perfect for cranky kids or a baby who needs a nap.

Temple Hall Farm Regional Park
15789 Temple Hall Lane
Leesburg, VA 20176
703-779-9372
www.nvrpa.org/park/temple_hall_farm

See Chapter 4: Zoos, Farms, and Pick-Your-Owns

Theodore Roosevelt Island
George Washington Pkwy
Arlington, VA 22216
www.nps.gov/this

See Chapter 3: Nature Centers

Turner Farm
Georgetown Pike & Springvale Road
Great Falls, VA 22066
703-388-2807
www.fairfaxcounty.gov/parks/turnerfarm

Have your little ones ever asked you "What's in the sky?" If so, take a trip to the Turner Farm for one of their educational programs. Located in Great Falls and run by the Fairfax County Park Authority, Turner Farms offers an array of activities for visitors including an educational astronomy program supported by the Analemma Society. Every Friday evening (weather permitting) local astronomers set up telescopes and offer an educational overview of the night's sky. Visitors are invited to bring a telescope of their own, a camera, a blanket and a snack for the event. No reservations are required. For day-trippers, there is a small playground, picnic area, port-o-johns, walking trails and lots of nature to view. The park is open from dawn until dusk daily with the exception of fair weather Fridays. Admission is free, but donations are welcome. No on-site staff is available for visitors. For small children, this venue is best when a special program or activity is planned.

Insider Tip: Equestrians are also fans of the park. The former dairy farm boasts 40-acres of open field riding as well as beginner level cross country courses. A large outdoor arena is free and open to the public. Unfortunately, horse rentals are not available. You must bring your own horse.

Upton Hill Regional Park
6060 Wilson Boulevard
Arlington, VA 22205
703-534-3437
www.nvrpa.org/park/upton_hill

See Chapter 7:Water Parks And Spraygrounds

Veterans Memorial Regional Park
14300 Featherstone Road
Woodbridge, VA 22191
703-491-2183
www.pwcparks.org

Veterans Memorial Regional Park has a diverse offering of outdoor amenities. The park has a large outdoor swimming pool with slide, baseball fields, a playground, a picnic pavilion, tennis courts and hiking trails. The park also boasts a Tony Hawk-worthy skate park with an 11-ft vert ramp drop and a 6,300 sq. ft. open-flow course. Outdoor basketball courts are free to use.

Indoor courts in the community center are used for open play basketball and soccer during the week and require a small fee. The park offers picnic pavilion rentals that come with access to a volleyball court, a horseshoe pit and barbecue grills. The community center offers classes for children, teens and adults as well as a children's playschool program for kids ages 3 - 5. Many of the outdoor areas in the park are not stroller friendly, including the picnic area. Admission is free, but there are fees for community center activities and picnic pavilion use rentals.

Insider Tip: Locals grumble that the venue isn't great for outdoor use with small children with its dated playground. Some also think the fees to use the picnic pavilion are excessive. Best to choose this venue for older children, a day at the pool or one of the community center services.

Chapter 3

Nature Centers

Chapter 3: Nature Centers

Audubon Naturalist Society-Rust Sanctuary
802 Children's Center Road
Leesburg, VA 20175
703-669-0000
www.audubonnaturalist.org

The Audubon Naturalist Society's Rust Sanctuary boasts 68-acres rich with meadows, forests, ponds, and even a sandpit for toddlers to play in. You may find nesting songbirds from the tropics in the oak-hickory forest and devilish dragonflies. The Audubon Naturalist Society offers families a unique opportunity to experience nature year round with programs such as Butterfly Strolls, Spring Frog Choruses and Turkey Tracks In The Snow. The Society also hosts a nature preschool and family, scout, school and camp programs. Eco-conscious parents can arrange a green birthday party that includes a nature lesson, hike and nature games like Wiggling Worm.

There is one trail leading to the pond that is stroller friendly. Other trails would require a rugged stroller or baby carrier. No admission fee is required and you can bring a picnic lunch. Restrooms are available when the facility's main house is open. Changing tables are not available. Check website or call for hours and more information.

Audubon Naturalist Society-Webb Sanctuary
12829 Chestnut Street
Clifton, VA 20124
703-803-8400
http://www.audubonnaturalist.org

The Audubon Naturalist Society's Webb Sanctuary has 20-acres that include a woodland, meadow and stream valley. Enjoy nesting songbirds from the tropics, amphibians, wood frogs, fox and other mammals. Reptiles such as turtles, five-lined skinks and black-rat snakes also call the Webb Nature Sanctuary home. Interpretive trail signs help guest learn about the local natural history. Parents and children can participate in fun programs like the Butterfly Stroll, Spring Frog Choruses and Turkey Tracks In The Snow. This venue is ideal for elementary school age children. A picnic area is available. Restrooms are NOT available. There is limited parking on site.

Broadlands Nature Center
21907 Claiborne Parkway
Broadlands, VA 20148
703-729-9704
www.broadlandshoa.org

Run by the Broadlands HOA, this charming nature center is located in the heart of the Broadlands community in Ashburn, VA. The Broadlands HOA, in conjunction with the Audubon Naturalist Society, provide a number of nature programs and classes that are open to the entire community. There are a number of seasonal nature programs for adults as well as children's programs. Little ones will enjoy the toddler and preschool programs that often incorporate the resident animals and reptiles including rabbits, snakes, birds, toads and a newt. The nature center's programs, pond and creek are popular for girl and boy scouts seeking wildlife badges. The venue can also be used for birthday parties. Program fees apply and are higher for non-residents. The center is open year-round. Hours vary. It is best to check the website for operational hours, center programs and registration details. The center has restrooms, a patio and picnic tables. The venue is stroller friendly and within walking distance to a playground.

Insider Tip: The Broadlands is large planned community with a number of restaurants in the area. Check web listings for Broadlands on sites such as www.yelp.com to choose from an array of family friendly restaurants.

Bull Run Mountains Conservancy
P.O. Box 210
Broad Run, VA 20137
703-753-2631
www.brmconservancy.org

Bull Run Mountains Conservancy is located on the southern 800-acres of Bull Run Mountain Natural Area Preserve. It is a quick 15 minutes from Manassas, Middleburg and Warrenton, VA. Founded in 1995, BRMC rests near the Occoquan and Goose Creek watersheds. Its location lends itself to family friendly programs including hikes, day-long nature camps and a number of youth programs. One of the biggest events of the year falls around Halloween and includes a safari and night hike.

Day-trippers will enjoy the lush scenery and nature inspired family events. BRMC also offers birthday adventures for members. There are a number of trails that are most suitable for school-age children. The venue is not considered stroller friendly. Family port-o-potties are available.

Insider Tip: The Bull Run Mountains Conservancy is the educational arm of the Bull Run Mountains Natural Area Preserve. They also maintain much of the public access facilities at the southern end of the preserve. For serious hikers and for older children, you can enjoy the 2,486-acres of woodlands, hiking trails, white quartzite cliffs and even a boulder field beneath the High Point Mountain. Designated a "Natural Area Preserve," Bull Run Mountains Natural Area Preserve boasts rare and unusual ecological features.

Ellanor C. Lawrence Park
5040 Walney Road
Chantilly, VA 20151
703-631-0013
www.fairfaxcounty.gov/parks/ecl

Ellanor C. Lawrence Park is home to the Walney Visitor Center. This public park offers family programs and educational exhibits. This is a popular destination for locals and hosts over 30,000 visitors annually. Children are taken to another world as they start their journey at the Walney Visitor Center, a converted 1780 farmhouse. Visitors can see live animal exhibits and historic exhibits. Younger children will enjoy the touch table area, greenhouse and classroom.

During your visit make sure to head over to the Middlegate Complex & Cabell's Mill. Set along Big Rocky Run near the meadow, the mill once served as a grist, sumac and sawmill. You will also find a beehive, a smokehouse, an Icehouse Ruin and Dairy Complex on the property. In addition, streams, meadows, and ponds abound in this picturesque Fairfax County park.

Pack a lunch and enjoy your morning, afternoon or day at this diverse park. Sports enthusiasts will enjoy the 4 miles of trails that are ideal for jogging, hiking, bird watching, and walking. Trails are not paved. You would need a solid stroller to navigate the trails. Open year-round, daily except Tuesdays. Admission is free and restrooms are available in the visitor center during business hours. Check website or call for hours and more information.

Insider Tip: Ellanor C. Lawrence Park also offers nature camps, field trips, birthday parties and scout programs.

Elizabeth Hartwell Mason Neck State Park Wildlife Refuge
7603 High Point Road
Lorton, VA 22079
703-490-4979
www.fws.gov/refuges

Located 18 south of Washington DC, this beautiful 2,227-acre refuge sits on the Potomac River on the Mason Neck peninsula. Run by the U.S. Fish & Wildlife Service, Mason Neck Park boasts the largest freshwater marsh in Northern Virginia and the largest Great Blue heron rookery in the region with over 1,400 nests and 4.4 miles of shoreline. Mason Neck was also named one of the "Top 10" sites in the country for watching Bald eagles.

With over 200 species of birds, 31 species of mammals and 44 species of reptiles and amphibians, this is a wonderful retreat for locals and visitors. The 285-acre Great Marsh is home to waterfowl, marsh wrens, green herons, and great egrets. White-tailed deer, eastern gray squirrel, red fox and an occasional flock of wild turkey are encountered on the refuges three hiking trails. Refuge trails are open dawn to dusk year round.

Be sure to bring comfortable clothes and walking shoes. While you can bring a pet, you must keep your pet on a 10ft leash at all times. You will need to bring waters bottles for your hikes. The terrain is not stroller friendly. Restrooms are available but are semi-permanent structures that do not have water. There is one ADA approved trail that could accommodate a stroller. This venue is more appropriate for elementary school age children.

Front Royal Fish Hatchery Station
Route 619
Strasburg, VA
540-635-5350
www.dgif.virginia.gov/fishing/stocking/hatcheries.asp

Operated by the Virginia Department of Game and Inland Fisheries, this hatchery is used for the production of walleye and smallmouth bass fingerlings and servers as a distribution point for trout, catfish and other species to the waters of northern and northwestern Virginia. Visitors are welcome to visit their ponds Monday through Friday. Kids will get a kick out of seeing all these fish up close and watching them churn up the water with their splashing. All visits are free. Call ahead to confirm hours.

Green Spring Gardens
4603 Green Spring Road
Alexandria, Virginia 22312
703-642-5173
www.fairfaxcounty.gov/parks/greenspring

Offering a wealth of information for the home gardener, Green Spring Gardens offers a whimsical children's garden, family workshops and popular "Garden Sprouts" preschool programs. The gardens feature a stunning assortment of trees, plants, and vegetables. Shop for plants, gardening tools, and gifts in the Horticultural Center. Also visit the historic Green Springs House museum for changing art exhibits, special programs, and teas.

Gulf Branch Nature Center
3608 N. Military Road
Arlington, VA 22207
703-228-3403
www.arlingtonva.us

Gulf Branch Nature Center is a part of the Arlington County Department of Parks and Recreation. It provides environmental education programs for all ages. Families can enjoy the exhibits, Kid's Discovery Room, the Pollinator Garden, live animal exhibits, a pond, a restored log cabin, and observation bee hive. Gulf Branch Nature Center also offers birthday parties for children. The venue has public restrooms, water fountains and is NOT wheelchair accessible. Admission is free, however, many of the events held at Gulf Branch Nature Center do require a small fee. Visit the county calendar and select the "Environment" category and applicable age group for classes and events.

Restrooms on site but there aren't any changing tables. Street parking is available. Only a few trails are stroller friendly. The short walk around the nature center is ideal for toddlers.

Insider Tip: Get the scoop through the Gulf Branch publication "The Snag" for family friendly events for school-aged children and for adult events. For preschoolers (ages 3-5) and tiny tots (ages 18-35 months), sign up for "The Snag for Wee Ones." Subscribe online for a quarterly e-mail notification.

Hidden Oaks Nature Center
7701 Royce Street
Annandale, VA 22003
703-931-1065
http://www.fairfaxcounty.gov/parks/hidden-oaks/

Hidden Oaks Nature Center sits on a 52-acre park that boasts an interactive exhibit for children two years and up. This family friendly venue has trails, creeks, butterfly gardens, and a nearby playground. Visitors can move from the idyllic park setting into the main building. Once inside you will discover live animal displays, a climbing "tree" loft stage that plays host to puppet shows, a resource library and a Urban Woodlands: Habitats and Havens interactive exhibit. At Nature Playce, children will hear birds singing and the gentle rustle of leaves in the trees. A small water feature reflects the open sky above. While parents relax on a bench in the serenity of the forested enclosure, kids can dig in moist dirt, make mud pies, feel the texture of tree bark and create a ground fort. Preschools and elementary grade classes, scouts and birthday parties are also welcome to visit Nature Playce as part of their park experience.

Hidden Pond Nature Center
8511 Greeley Boulevard
Springfield, VA 22152
703-451-9588
www.fairfaxcounty.gov/parks/hiddenpond

Hidden Pond Nature Center is part of the Fairfax County Parks system and features an accessible nature center with fish, amphibians, and reptiles. Inside there are also hands on games, puzzles, and fossils for children to explore. The nature center hosts a variety of programs throughout the year for kids ages 3-12. Outside the nature center, take a stroll around the pond, or a longer hike on one of the adjacent trails connecting the pond to the 700-acre Pohick Stream Valley Park system. A nice wooden playground featuring slides, tunnels, ramps, and monkey bars is located near the parking lot. Bathroom facilities with changing table are located in the nature center, and a limited selection of snacks and drinks are also available for sale. Check website or call for hours and more information.

Insider Tip: The playground is located in direct sunlight, but the picnic tables are in the shade. There is also a shaded picnic pavilion is located behind the nature center overlooking the pond. Check out turtles in the pond or participate in catch and release fishing.

Jerome "Buddie" Ford Nature Center
5750 Sanger Avenue
Alexandria, VA 22311
703-746-5559
www.alexandriava.gov

The City of Alexandria's Jerome "Buddie" Ford Nature Center offers year-round exhibits including live reptiles, an aquarium with native fish species, and a greenhouse with tropical rainforest plants. Enjoy the small library with a children's section. There are also games and fun activities for kids of all ages. Restrooms are available. The venue is stroller friendly.

Classes, camps and programs are offered throughout the year. Small fees apply to some classes with larger fees for camps, afterschool programs and birthday parties. The facility is open from Wednesday - Sunday with varied hours and closed on Monday & Tuesday. Check website or call for hours and more information at www.alexandriava.gov.

Insider Tip: Steps from the nature center sits the Dora Kelley Nature Park, a 50-acre wildlife sanctuary with a mile long nature trail that boasts woodlands, streams, hills, and marshland. Guests can take advantage of guided tours of the park with groups of eight or more (reservations required). An ADA accessible (stroller friendly) paved bike trail runs through the park.

Long Branch Nature Center
625 S. Carlin Springs Road
Arlington, VA 22204
703-228-6535
www.arlingtonva.us

Run by Arlington County, Long Branch has long been a favorite of locals. Set in an idyllic park setting, the nature center is family friendly and offers a multitude of environmental educational classes for children of all ages as well as adults. The venue has on site and off street parking but the spots fill up quickly during the summer and weekends.

Visitors will enjoy exhibits, animal displays, gardens, a pond and a fun Discovery Room for children. There are a number of paved trails for strollers and restrooms are available. Long Branch offers a useful online calendar that allows guests to view upcoming programs. Check website or call for hours and more information.

Meadowlark Gardens
9750 Meadowlark Gardens Court
Vienna, VA 22182
703-255-3631
www.nvrpa.org/park/meadowlark_botanical_gardens

Part of the Northern Virginia Regional Parks system, Meadowlark Gardens is a true hidden treasure. Nestled on 95-acres in suburban Vienna, Meadowlark Gardens is charming destination that will appeal to the entire family. Children of all ages can journey through the sprawling complex that boasts walking trails, lakes, native wildflowers, birds, butterflies as well as a beautiful seasonal offering of plants and trees. Meadowlark also hosts concerts, tours, field trips and workshops.

Meadowlark Gardens is open year round. There is a beautiful visitor centers that greets guests at the property entrance. Restrooms are available for visitors. The venue is closed on Thanksgiving Day, Christmas Day, New Year's

Day and when snow or ice covers the trails. All facilities on the property and most of the garden trails are designed in accordance with ADA standards. While visiting be sure enjoy the picnic area that sits beside the Gardens. Admission fees apply.

Insider Tip: Parent's groups routinely visit this idyllic setting for playdates and picnic time. Spring and fall are a gorgeous time to visit Meadowlark Garden. To protect the gardens, be sure to picnic only in designated areas and stay on designated paths.

Occoquan Bay National Wildlife Refuge
13950 Dawson Beach Road
Woodbridge, VA 22191
703-490-4979
www.fws.gov/refuges

Part of the Potomac River National Wildlife Refuge Complex, this 644-acre refuge is an enticing destination for children and adults. The wetlands, forest, woodlands, freshwater marshes and meadows will intrigue young naturalists. There is a diverse and robust offering of wildlife that includes over 220 species of birds, 600+ species of plant and 65 species of butterflies fill the refuge. The spring and fall bring migrating birds and raptors.

There are 4 miles of trails, all dirt. Visitors can take advantage of a two-mile wildlife drive. While the terrain is not stroller friendly, you can navigate the trails with an infant carrier. Restrooms are available. Most restrooms are semi-permanent. The main facility, when open, has two changing stations. A small fee is charged for admission. The refuge is opened year-round with varied hours. Check website or call for hours and more information.

Potomac Overlook Regional Park
2845 N. Marcey Road
Arlington, VA 22207
703-528-5406
www.nvrpa.org/park/potomac_overlook

Run by the Northern Virginia Regional Parks system, Potomac Overlook Regional Park is located in North Arlington on the Potomac Palisades. Visitors are welcome to enjoy the lush 70-acre park filled with woodland trails, inviting gardens, and a small picnic area.

The Nature Center offers visitors and innovative program called "Energerium". "Energerium" is fun and lively program that offers a unique way to learn the about ecology, Earth Science, physics, chemistry and shows how humans interact with natures elements. This interactive display is ideal for elementary and high school age children.

For smaller children, families will enjoy the live animals and natural history exhibits. There is also a live beehive display and a Kids Cave where visitors can learn about the bats. Birthday parties and summer camps are available.

Restrooms are available at the main center and shelter station. Visitors enjoy ample parking but spots do fill up on the weekends. One trail is stroller friendly but elevations make other trails more difficult to navigate. The venue has a diverse offering for toddlers through seniors with varied trails for all age groups. Despite the name, there isn't an overlook that allows visitors to view the Potomac River. You must go down one of the trails to see the Potomac River. The Nature Center is open to the general public Tuesday through Sunday and is closed on Mondays. Call to confirm current operational hours.

Riverbend Park
8700 Potomac Hills Street,
Great Falls, VA 22066
703-759-9018
www.fairfaxcounty.gov/parks/riverbend

When visiting Riverbend Park guests are treated to over 400 gorgeous acres of meadows, forests, and ponds. This park has it all: boating, fishing, gorgeous river views, wildflowers and birds.

With a diverse network of over 10 miles of trails, visitors can pick the level of difficulty and length of a hike. Don't be surprised to see horses and mountain bikers join in the fun. In addition to a scenic walk or hike, you can also take advantage of classes, programs, and tours for that appeal to all ages.

The main picnic area near the visitor center is an ideal spot for a family picnic. Grills are provided and trees shade guests from the hot summer sun. Admission is free and restrooms are available at the visitor center. While the Paw Paw trail is stroller friendly, most of the trails will not accommodate a stroller. The park is open daily from 7am to dusk. Check website or call for hours and more information.

Insider Tip: Riverbend Parks offers some very cool birthday party ideas including Fishing Fun and Nature Birthdays for children as young as 3 years of age. In addition, Riverbend Park hosts the annual Virginia Indian Festival!

Theodore Roosevelt Island
George Washington Pkwy
Arlington, VA 22216
www.nps.gov/this

Run by the National Park Service, Theodore Roosevelt Island was built as a tribute to our 26th President. From the moment you step off the footbridge onto the island you are immediately transported to a naturalist's paradise. Guests enjoy nature trails and a boardwalk that allows guests to become enveloped by a lush scenery of forests, swamp and wildlife. Your journey will take you past the Theodore Roosevelt Memorial where you can learn more about Roosevelt's rich legacy and commitment to conservation.

With three trails ranging in distance from .4 miles to 1.3 miles, the terrain is manageable for young children. Some, but not all of the trails will accommodate a stroller. While little ones should be able to navigate the trails, parents should be vigilant to ensure that small children do not fall off the boardwalk or get too far off the beaten path.

Admission is free and limited parking is available on a first come, first serve basis. Expect a busy parking lot on weekends. You could opt to park at Gravelly Point and bike to the island. Semi-permanent restrooms are available. Theodore Roosevelt Island is open daily from 6 a.m. until 10 p.m. year round.

Insider Tip: Theodore Roosevelt Island is located directly off the Mount Vernon Trail. While bicycling is not permitted on the island there is a bicycle rack located in the parking lot area next to the Mount Vernon Trail.

Walker Nature Education Center
11450 Glade Drive
Reston, VA 20191
703-476-9689
www.reston.org

The Walker Nature Education Center is an ideal destination for children of all ages. This 72-acre nature center offers year-round access to 2 miles of trails, a stroller-friendly Native Plant Trail, a hardwood forest, pond, campfire rings, a picnic pavilion and a Nature House. Families can also take advantage of a number of programs for children ranging in age from 18 months through 12 years of age including: All Ages Programs, Babes in the Woods, Preschool Happenings, Children's Birthday Programs, Scout Programs and School Programs. Most programs require a small fee and reservations are required. The Nature House is open every day except Tuesday. Restrooms and free parking are available.

Chapter 4

Zoos, Farms, and Pick-Your-Own

Chapter 4: Zoos, Farms, and Pick-Your-Own

Belvedere Plantation
1410 Belvedere Drive
Fredricksburg, VA 22408
540-373-4478
www.belvedereplantation.com

A working farm with crops such as wheat, corn, soybeans, and pumpkins, this farm is best known for its gigantic Harvest Festival in the fall. For a fee, guests can enjoy hayrides, a giant cornfield maze, pumpkin picking, bonfires, farm animals, pedal carts, pig racing, and more. The parking lot includes picnic facilities, but outside food is not allowed in the farm. To eat, visit the Red Rooster Restaurant for fast food fare, barbecue sandwiches, and snacks. The Plantation Market sells handmade gifts, decorations, jellies, and pumpkin carving accessories. Fresh pies, fudge, and cider are for sale in the bakery. Group and birthday party packages are available.

Insider Tip: Take a few dollars off your admission by becoming a free email subscriber or fan on Facebook.

(The) Children's Farm
14807 Bristow Road
Manassas, VA 20112
703-792-6465
www.pwcgov.org

Located near the animal shelter, this hidden gem is often passed by. Here visitors can experience animals such as sheep, chickens, turkeys, goats, pigs, and peacocks. Admission is free. At the time of publication, the Children's Farm is only open on Thursdays, from noon to 4 p.m., weather permitting. Please call ahead to find out about special programs, tours, and additional hours of operation.

Claude Moore Colonial Farm
6310 Georgetown Pike
McLean, VA 22101
703-442-7557
www.1771.org

Step back time and visit with the Bradley's, a fictional family living on a farm in 1771. Watch as the family goes about their daily life, do farm chores, plant and harvest crops, and eat together as a family. Each season, a special colonial market fair is offered with colonial food and products for sale. On select days, kids ages four and up can also experience farm skill programs and participate in games, crafts, and activities. Other special events such as "Chew the Fat" (candle and soap making) and "Wassail" (cider and holiday games) are popular with local families. Registration is required for some programs, so please call ahead or check the website.

Cox Farms
15621 Braddock Road
Centreville, VA 20120
703-830-4121
www.coxfarms.com

Home of the biggest fall festival in Northern Virginia, this is a popular family-friendly attraction with year round special events and fun, including an Easter Egg Hunt, Mother's Day event, Fall Festival, Pumpkin Madness (pumpkin stomping and crushing) and Winter Holiday events. Visit animals such as llamas, chickens, alpacas, rabbits, goat, and sheep and shop the popular Corner Market featuring fresh farm produce. Of course, the Fall Festival is the main event and is huge. The famous not-so scary hayride through woods and fields amuses visitors of all ages. There are also giant slides, live entertainment (on the weekends,) a corn maze, goat run, farm animals, tire swings, tunnels, climbing structures and many more attractions. Food is available for purchase. Kids over twelve and teens may want to check out the "Field of Fears" offered during certain fall evenings. Check the website for latest events and details.

Insider Tip: On the fall weekends, the festival can get crowded. Plan to show up early, even fifteen to thirty minutes before opening time. Head straight to the hayride before the lines get too long.

Frying Pan Park's Kidwell Farm
2709 West Ox Road
Herndon, VA 20171
703-437-9101
www.fairfaxcounty.gov/parks/fryingpanpark/

Part of the Fairfax County Park system, this farm boasts a variety of features and admission is free. Kids can interact with farm animals such as horses, cattle, sheep, goats, pigs, ducks, chickens, turkeys, and peacocks. The animals are spread out in various barns, pastures, and pens and farm buildings also include a 1930's farmhouse, apple cider press, smokehouse, and blacksmith. In addition to the farm, there is a tractor ride (fee and weather permitting,) antique carousel (fee and weather permitting,) visitors center museum, playground, and country farm store which sells local products, farm related toys, and a variety of gifts. The Equestrian facilities include public outdoor riding trails and jumps and a huge, indoor arena with shows and exhibits throughout the year. Frying Pan Farm Park is also the site of the Fairfax County 4H Fair and Carnival, musical entertainment series, and a seasonal farmers' market. There is always a special event going on at Frying Pan Farm Park, and popular weekly classes like "Little Hands on the Farm" fill up quickly.

Great Country Farms
18780 Foggy Bottom Road
Bluemont, Virginia 20135
540-554-2073
www.greatcountryfarms.com

This Loudoun County family favorite features barnyard animals, a giant jumping pillow, corn mazes, playgrounds, slides, gem mining, a hayride, and a cow train. Many seasonal festivals are offered at the farm and u-pick produce is extremely popular. On weekends, the "Roosterant" sells lunches and snacks and is now concentrating on serving all natural meat products. The farm store sells unique gifts and food products. Plan to spend at least a half-day to see everything. Check website for up to date information about admission fees, special events, and hours.

Insider Tip: Happy parents will also like that a free wine tasting at Bluemont Vineyards, located across the street, is included in the farm admission.

Hartland Orchard
P.O. Box 124
3064 Hartland Lane
Markham, VA 22643
540-364-2316
www.hartlandorchard.com
www.hartlandfarmandorchard.com (for Fall Festival)

Hartland Orchard is farm that offers seasonal pick-your-own produce such as strawberries, cherries, peaches, apples, pumpkins, and cut your own Christmas trees. Their apple crops are known as some of the best in the region. During weekends in the fall, the fall festival includes a corn maze, hayrides, a jumping pillow, and giant slides. It is always a good idea to call before you visit.

Leesburg Animal Park
19270 James Monroe Highway
Leesburg, VA 20175
703-433-0002
www.leesburganimalpark.com

This 21-acre zoo is home to a variety of farm, petting and exotic animals. Represented species include llamas, goats, sheep, deer, donkeys, zebras, camels, porcupines, lemurs, and more. Besides touring the exhibits, other activities include wagon rides, pony rides, live animal encounters, a moon bounce and a playground. Special events and shows are scheduled in the summer months. During the fall, Leesburg Animal Park is home to the popular "Pumpkinville" attraction, one of Loudoun County's premier fall festivals. Pumpkinville includes mazes, hayrides, giant slides, apple cider, moon bounces, and of course, pumpkins. Ticket sales are available online.

Insider Tip: Coupons for Leesburg Animal Park and the seasonal Pumpkinville are frequently offered online at the Leesburg Animal Park website and on daily deal sites. Keep a lookout!

Luray Zoo & Reptile Center
1087 US Highway 211
West Luray, VA 22835
540-743-4113
www.lurayzoo.com

The only privately-owned rescue zoo in Virginia, Luray Zoo provides homes for over 250 animals including unusual reptiles, skunks, tigers, porcupines, wallabies, yaks, and more. The petting zoo is popular with children and allows kids to pet, feed, and groom different animals. During the summer, regular animal shows and performances are scheduled. Visit the website for information regarding admission, operating hours, current exhibits, and directions. The website will also show the schedule for the animal shows and performances, which can be the highlight of the visit.

Insider Tip: You can combine a trip with the nearby Luray Caverns by arriving at the Caverns early and then heading over to the Luray Zoo after lunch.

Old Mine Ranch
17504 Mine Road
Dumfries, VA 22025
703-441-1382
www.oldmineranch.net

This working farm adjoins Prince William Forest Park. Admission includes a pony ride for each child, train ride, hayride, moon bounce, and food to feed the farm animals. Seasonal activities include a sleigh ride with cookie decorating and hot cocoa in the winter and a pumpkin patch and haunted ghost town in the fall. Picnic facilities are available. Please note that during certain times of the year, the farm is only open on weekends. Always call ahead for the latest information.

Reston Zoo
1228 Hunter Mill Road
Vienna, VA 22182
703-757-6222
www.restonzoo.com

Located minutes from Reston Town Center, the Reston Zoo contains exotic animals such as monkeys, kangaroos, alligator, and tortoises. Children are able to purchase animal feed in the gift shop for the barnyard animals: sheep, goats, pigs, llamas, and geese. Admission includes a wild side wagon ride where visitors can view antelope, buffalo, ostrich, camels, zebras, and more. Special events, such as Boo at the Zoo for Halloween and children's entertainment in the summer, are offered throughout the year.

Insider Tip: The zoo features a picnic area and sells snacks and beverages, but another fun option is going up the road to Reston Town Center, filled with lots of shops and restaurants. Also, be warned that if you purchase the animal feed, certain geese and barnyard animals may continue to follow you around the grounds. This frightens some kids, but you know your child best!

Temple Hall Farm
15855 Limestone School Road
Leesburg, VA 20176
703-779-9372
www.nvrpa.org/park/temple_hall_farm/

Temple Hall Farm is a working farm dedicated to displaying the agricultural history of Loudoun County. From April through November, it is free to visit the farm. Families can view cows, chickens, pigs, sheep, goats, and even draft horses in the barns and pastures. On weekends, farm interpreters are available for free guided tours. The brand new visitor center contains maps, event brochures, public restrooms, and a multi-purpose room that is available to rent out for birthday parties and other functions.

Insider Tip: Thousands of area visitors come in the fall for the corn MAiZE (maze) and fall festival. Visit during this special time and experience a giant jumping pillow, cow train, pig races, pumpkin patch, hayrides, and more. The fall festival has its own website here.

Ticonderoga Farm
26175 Ticonderoga Road
Chantilly, VA 20152
703-327-4424
www.ticonderoga.com

A family farm located on the border of Loudoun and Fairfax County, this special place includes seasonal pick-your-own produce and fun attractions for the whole family. The Fairview Grounds has activities such as a cow train, hayrides, petting farm animals, giant jumping pillow, hillside slides, a bamboo maze, and more. Note that some attractions are only open on the weekends. Seasonal events, such as the Spring Easter Festival, Summer Harvest Festival, Fall Pumpkin Festival, and Winter Christmas Festival offer even more attractions and fun. Fresh produce, honey made on the grounds, free-range eggs, jams, and firewood can be purchased at the farm market. Concessions such as hot dogs, pizza, turkey legs, and snacks are sold on weekends.

Wegmeyer Farms
38299 Hughesville Road
Hamilton, Virginia 20158
540-364-2316
http://www.wegmeyerfarms.com/

Wegmeyer Farms is a pick-your-own farm that offers strawberries, raspberries, and blackberries in the spring/summer months and lots of variety of pumpkins in the fall. Please call ahead for operating hours and crop availability.

Insider Tip: Families that want to frequent the farm can join the PYO Club which offers members a complimentary discount and priority picking days.

Yankey Farms
14714 Vint Hill Road
Nokesville, VA 20181
703-618-3782
www.yankeyfarms.com

Yankey Farms is a fresh market produce farm located in Prince William County. During the late spring and early summer, pick your own strawberries is offered at the Vint Hill Road location. During the fall, this location turns into a pumpkin patch. Fall time at Yankey Farms also includes a corn maze, cow train, and a picnic area. Seasonal produce is for sale at the farm stand year round.

More Pick-Your-Own Farms (* Featured Produce)

Burnside Farms
4905 James Madison Highway
Haymarket, VA 20169
703-930-3052
www.burnsidefarms.com

* Tulips

Crooked Run Orchard
37883 East Main Street
Purcellville, VA 20132
(540) 338-6642
www.crookedrunorchard.com

* Asparagus, salad mixes, spinach, cherries, flowers, herbs, blackberries, peaches, raspberries, apples, pumpkins, and gourds

Eagletree Farm & Vineyard
15126 Harrison Hill Lane
Leesburg VA 20176
703-777-5954
www.eagletreefarm.com

*Blueberries

Evergreen Acres
2801 Hazelwood Drive
Nokesville, VA 20181
703-594-333
www.evergreenacres.biz

*Tomatoes, pumpkins, Christmas trees

Field of Flowers
7879 Allder School Road
Purcellville VA 20132
540-338-7231
www.fields-of-flowers.com

*Many varieties of flowers

Green Truck Farm
3015 Hartland Lane
Markham, VA 22643
540-316-7715
http://www.greentruckfarms.com/

*Strawberries, raspberries, spring vegetables, blackberries, pumpkins

Hollin Farms
11324 Pearlstone Lane
Delaplane, VA 20144
540-592-3701
www.hollinfarms.com

* Berries, greens, plums, cucumbers, pears, tomatoes, corn, eggplant, squash, apples, pumpkins, potatoes, peanuts, and more

Stribling Orchard
11587 Poverty Hollow Lane
Markham, VA 22643
540-364-3040
www.striblingorchard.com

*Peaches and Apples

Chapter 5

Playrooms, Bouncing, and Climbing

Chapter 5: Playrooms, Bouncing, and Climbing

Alexandria Soft Playroom
3210 King Street
Alexandria, VA
703-746-5553
www.alexandriava.gov

For a small fee, this soft playroom, located in the Chinquapin Recreation Center, offers a great place for toddlers to burn off energy in inclement weather. The playroom includes lots of soft wedges, mats, cylinders, and slides for little ones to climb on and build. The playroom is open daily, but please call ahead in case it is scheduled for a birthday party, event, or cleaning. There is a maximum number of 16 kids allowed in the play area, and socks must be worn.

Barcroft Sports and Fitness Center
4200 S. Four Mile Run
Arlington, VA 22206
703-228-0701
www.arlingtonva.us

Twice a week for a small fee, children under 5 can participate in a fun, indoor, drop-in playgroup. Fun toys are spread throughout the open gym floor, and children are encouraged to bring their own riding toys too. Please visit the website and call ahead regarding current times, cost, and guidelines.

Burke Racquet & Swim Club
6001 Burke Commons Road
Burke, VA 22015
703-250-1299
www.burkeclub.com

The Sport Climbing and the Exergym at Burke Racquet & Swim Club are open to non-members on Saturday and Sunday and by reservation Monday-Friday. The auto-belay climbing walls at Burke provide a great introduction to climbing for beginners and exhilarating challenges for more experienced climbers. Climbers must be at least 5 years old. The adjacent Exergym includes innovative full body computer games that incorporate fitness, eye-hand coordination, core strength training, agility and more into physical play. Participants must be at least 6 years old to use the Exergym.

Chibis Indoor Playground
44675 Cape Court, Suite 175
Ashburn, VA 20147
571-918-0301
www.chibisindoorplayground.com

Take off your shoes (but leave on your socks) and join the fun at one of the area's newest indoor playgrounds. Parents can play with their children in this safe, clean, indoor environment or take advantage of the lounge seating, free Wi-Fi, and socialize with other adults. The large playground is complete with slides, tunnels, and climbing structures. An infant playground has structures such as tunnels, a little house, and buckets of toys for sitters and walkers. Additional features such as a block center, train table, pretend kitchen area, and smaller climbing structures bring more fun for children of various age groups. Chibis continues to get rave reviews in the area and is becoming a local favorite. Recommended for children under seven.

Chuck E. Cheese
Multiple Locations in Northern Virginia
www.chuckecheese.com

With seven locations in Northern Virginia, Chuck E. Cheese offers arcade games, simulator rides, kiddie rides, and climbing structures. Activities vary by location. Find the location nearest you on the website. Food is available for purchase.

Falls Church Community Center
223 Little Falls Street
Falls Church, VA 22046
703-248-5077
www.fallschurchva.gov

Open gym is scheduled during the school year once a week for little ones under 5. The community center supplies some tunnels, soft climbing wedges, and riding toys, but children are also able to bring their own riding toys. Please call ahead for current date and time offerings.

Gymboree
Alexandria, Burke, Chantilly and Woodbridge
www.gymboreeclasses.com

Besides offering a nationally renowned gym class program for babies through school age children, many Gymboree locations also offer drop in playtimes.

House of Bounce
9404 Center Point Lane
Manassas, VA 20110
703-257-0777
www.houseofbounceva.com

This huge 6,400 square foot indoor play area offers fun for children of various ages. Kids enjoy bouncing on the supersized inflatables, and adults can take advantage of the complimentary coffee or soft drink during open bounce times. However, this place is so fun that adults may want to bounce along with their children too!

Jump-N-Jimmy's
6614 James Madison Highway
Haymarket, VA 20169
703 754-6822
www.jnjparty.com

The facility at Jump-N-Jimmy's hosts open bounce hours on giant inflatables, youth sports events, and great birthday parties. Locals in the Haymarket/Gainesville area may want to take advantage of the Frequent Bounce Pass. Socks are required on the bounce equipment, and parents must sign a waiver. Always call ahead for open bounce times, and check the website for special classes and events.

Jumping Jack Sports
44710 Cape Court
Ashburn, VA 20147
703-858-9901
www.jumpingjacksports.com

Here kids can zoom through a 70 foot inflatable obstacle course, climb on a giant cargo net, traverse a rock wall, and participate in interactive dance and exercise games in the XRKade. For younger children ages 3-6, special Mom's Morning Out and Kid's Afternoon Out drop off programs are available weekly. Other classes and events for kids include a Girls' Power Hour, Mega Sports Sampler classes, and Family Olympics. Open gym times are open throughout the week. Please call ahead as times sometimes vary from listed on their website.

JW Tumbles
Alexandria, Arlington, Ashburn and Herndon
www.jwtumbles.com

With locations in Alexandria, Arlington, Ashburn, and Herndon, JW Tumbles offers exciting exercise, gymnastics, and indoor playground classes for kids 4 months old through 9 years. Non-members can take advantage of regularly scheduled open play times (for a fee.) Adults must supervise and remain in the facility with their children.

JWT Playzone
2499 N. Harrison Street
Arlington, VA 22207
703-531-1470
www.arlington.jwtumbles.com

We all know JW Tumbles offers great award-winning growth development programs, but did you know that they offer a soft-play area? JWT Playzone is located in Arlington, VA next to JW Tumbles gym. Kids will find tunnels, slides as well as tons of stuff to climb under, over and through. Sometimes the Playzone is scheduled for parties and playgroups. Call ahead for open play availability.

Kidz in Motion
Woodbridge and Fredricksburg
www.kidsnmotion.biz

This locally owned bounce-house business is a favorite for area birthday parties and open play sessions. Each location includes big inflatables and safe indoor playground equipment/climbing structures. The Woodbridge location also features a Mini-Gym for toddlers and preschoolers with regularly scheduled movement classes. Special events and parents' night out are offered throughout the year. Check the website and call the location nearest you for the latest updates and schedule.

Kneehigh Ninja
1136 West Broad Street
Falls Church, VA 22046
703-237-7433
www.kneehighninja.com

Children four and under can enjoy themselves in the indoor playground at Kneehigh Ninja that opens to the public from October-March a couple of mornings a week. The padded room includes mats and soft climb-on and building structures. Reservations are guaranteed by pre-payment through PayPal on the Kneehigh Ninja website. Walk-ins are only accepted if there is availability.

Lee District REC Center
6601 Telegraph Road
Franconia, VA 22310
703-922-9841
www.fairfaxcounty.gov

During open play times, the soft playroom at Lee District Recreation Center is a fun haven for little ones with a ball pit and movable, soft climbing toys and small tunnels and slides. For a small fee, toddlers will enjoy this indoor playroom. Sometimes the playroom is closed for a birthday party or an event. Always call ahead to check availability.

Little Gym (The)
Ashburn, Alexandria Huntley Meadows, Alexandria Van Dorn, Fairfax, Falls Church, Gainesville
www.thelittlegym.com

A popular location for preschool movement and gymnastic classes, many area The Little Gym locations offer open playtimes for non-members.

Lubber Run Community Center
300 N. Park Drive
Arlington, VA 22203
703-228-4712
www.arlingtonva.us

From October through May, children under five can explore the open gym/indoor playground at Lubber Run a few times a week. Participants are encouraged to bring a ride on toy or tricycle from home. Payment is cash only. Schedule is listed on the website.

Majestic Fun/ Luxe Events
8490 Centreville Road
Manassas, VA 20111
571-292-2157
www.majesticfun.com

This restaurant is filled with an indoor obstacle course, moon bounces, slides, arcade games, billiards and more. The venue offers parties for adults and children alike and has open play times. Food includes homemade pizza, subs, wings, and hot dogs. Visit the website for hours and additional information.

MuBu Kids
442 S Washington Street
Falls Church, VA 22046
703-241-PLAY
www.mobukids.com

An independently owned studio, MuBu Kids is a local favorite for indoor fun! It is the first studio in Northern Virginia featuring custom-made soft foam climbing structures and also contains a fun tree house and soft, movable mats and blocks. Besides offering open play, the MuBu Kids studio has award winning movement, music, dance classes, and birthday parties.

My Gym
Alexandria, Burke & Chantilly
www.mygym.com

Primarily a studio for movement and gymnastics classes for babies through school-aged kids, most Northern Virginia My Gym locations offer open play times where non-members can drop in (for a fee) and experience the studios' climbing structures, ball pits, gymnastics equipment, and more.

nZone
14550 Lee Road
Chantilly, VA 20151
703-226-0118
www.thenzone.com

The nZone is an indoor sports and athletic field center. There are youth clinics, camps, classes, and birthday parties. Special events are scheduled throughout the year.

Parenting Playgroups
Falls Church and Alexandria
www.parentingplaygroups.com

Parents and children can interact together and meet new friends in the weekly drop-in play in the Parenting Playgroups preschool classroom, which contains arts and craft supplies, toys, and fun preschool materials. In addition to this open play, Parenting Playgroups is well known for its parent education classes, camps, and preschool classes.

PB and Jack
9540 Main Street
Fairfax VA 22031
703-865-7773
www.pbandjack.com

The newest indoor playspace in Fairfax County, PB and Jack is a place where "kids can be kids, and adults can be adults." Kids can play in the soft indoor playzone complete with ocean-themed climbing structures, slides, an infant zone, and lego building area. Adults can take advantage of the cafe featuring gourmet coffee drinks, free WiFi, and snacks all while viewing their children. The play area is staffed with experienced employees that have fun playing and interacting with the children. Besides the open play, the place offers different studio rooms that host music, art, movement, dance, and language classes for kids, as well as fitness and art classes for adults. Visit the website for special events, pricing, and the latest updates.

Play N' Learn Playground Superstore
4102 Pepsi Place
Chantilly, VA 20151
703-502-1864
www.playnlearn.com

Kids ages eight and under can drop in during free open play sessions and climb on the many indoor playgrounds, go down the slides, jump on the trampolines, and more. This is actually a playground showroom that sells playground equipment.

Pump It Up
Leesburg and Manassas
www.pumpitupparty.com

This bounce house franchise has locations in Manassas and Leesburg. Kids can get their energy out by jumping and climbing on the giant inflatables during open play times. Special parents' night out programs, camps, and birthday parties are also offered.

Rebounderz
22400 Davis Drive
Sterling, VA 20164
703-433-5867
www.rebounderz.com

This growing franchise offers "extreme" jumping for adults and children. Participants wear helmets and special soft shoes (provided by Rebounderz) and are set loose in giant areas of floor and wall trampolines and foam pits. In addition to the 12,000 square feet of rebounding surface, Rebounderz offers food concessions, video arcade games, and parties.

Sport Bounce of Loudoun
44710 Cape Court
Ashburn, VA 20147
703- 729-9522
www.sportbounce.com

A gigantic 10,000 square foot facility filled with giant inflatables and moon bounces. Open bounces are scheduled throughout the week, as well as Junior Jumpers for ages 18 months old to 5 years. Check the website for information about birthday parties, schedules, and special events.

SportRock Climbing Centers
www.sportrock.com

SportRock offers huge climbing walls with lots of programs for kids including summer camps, kids' night, open climbing, birthday parties, climbing teams, and scout programs. SportRock has locations in Alexandria and Sterling.

Sprout at Saffron
3260 Wilson Boulevard
Arlington, VA 22201
703-276-2355
www.sproutatsaffron.com

Designed to be a safe haven for families, children can enjoy open playtime while their caregiver visits the cafe, relaxes in the meditation room, takes a yoga/fitness class, or even takes a nap! Sprout also offers music, movement and yoga classes for children of various ages. The open play times are designed for children under six, and the room is filled with educational toys and art materials. The location in Clarendon makes it metro accessible and close to lots of area shops and restaurants.

Urban Evolution
Alexandria and Manassas
www.urbanevo.com

This "alternative" gym offers parkour and urban fitness for older kids and adults. In this fun environment, participants can climb, bounce, and challenge themselves on the elements. See the website for details and descriptions.

Vertical Rock Climbing
10225 Nokesville Road
Manassas, VA 20110
855-822-5462
http://climb-va.com

A rock climbing venue with an insane amount of climbing routes offered for a variety of abilities. Vertical Rock Climbing in Manassas has classes, drop in climbing, kids' nights, and climbing teams. Birthday parties and special deals for groups, such as scouts are available. Recommended for ages 6 through adult.

Chapter 6

Malls With Indoor Play Spaces

Chapter 6: Malls with Indoor Play Spaces

Dulles Town Center
21100 Dulles Town Circle
Dulles, VA 20166
703-404-7120
www.shopdullestowncenter.com

Keeping with the Dulles theme, this play area includes a big, climb on airplane with sliding components, a control tower tunnel, a baggage cart structure that kids can climb on and pretend to drive, and some ramps. The play area is only open to children under 42 inches. Other entertainment for kids, at the mall, includes an express train ride and an indoor vintage carousel. Information about both, including current location, operating cost, and hours can be found here: www.shopdullestowncenter.com/info/express.

Insider Tip: Local and national tot rock favorites perform free concerts regularly at the mall by Sears. Check the website or sign up for the kids' club email list for the latest updates.

Fair Oaks Mall
11750 Fair Oaks Mall
Fairfax, VA 22030
703-359-8300
www.shopfairoaksmall.com

The Fair Oaks Mall enclosed play area is themed after the Looney Tunes Express, including favorite characters like Bugs Bunny and Tweety Bird. The floor is a soft, springboard material, and structures include a climbing train, small triangle slide, tunnels, and climb on characters. Some of the structures make noises or give off lights when touched. Benches for the parents border the area, making it easy to watch your child. The area can get crowded and is best for children under 5.

Landmark Mall
5801 Duke Street
Alexandria, VA 22304
703-354-8405
www.landmarkmall.com

Compared to the other giants in the area, Landmark Mall itself is a small-scale shopping mall, but does have some large feature department stores and other favorites. This woodland themed play area is great for crawlers and new walkers. The floor is a soft springboard, but not enclosed. Little ones will love the log tunnels and lights. Recommended for toddlers and older infants.

Manassas Mall
8300 Sudley Road - Suite M1
Manassas, VA 20109
703-368-7232
www.manassasmall.com/kids_at.aspx

The brand new soft play area just opened in the JCPenney court in early 2013. There is a woodland theme with a bridge, tree slide, log tunnel, and some creatures and flowers to climb on. The monthly "Movers and Shakers" club features free performances by local tot rock favorites like Mr. Don and Peter McCory. The schedule is listed online.

Potomac Mills Mall
2700 Potomac Mills Circle
Woodbridge, VA 22192
703-496-9301
www.simon.com/mall/default.aspx?id=1260

Located in the mall's neighborhood 2 by TJ Maxx, this Virginia themed play area opened in early 2012. Climbing structures include George Washington and his fabled cherry tree, Monticello, Chesapeake blue crabs, a cardinal (Virginia's state bird,) a pretend ship, a cannon, and more. There are games and mirrors along the wall for little ones, as well as small slides. Please note that the maximum height requirement to play in the area is 48". This colorful new play area is sure to be fun for little ones when the weather is less than ideal! Potomac Mills offers special free entertainment and events for kids that are hosted by the "Simon Kidgits Club" throughout the year. Join the Simon Kidgits Club to get news about Kidgits Club events, free take-aways, complimentary refreshments from Starbucks and Rita's Ice, and a free T-shirt.

Insider Tip: Potomac Mills is a large mall with endless retail shops and a number of food options. With such large terrain to cover it is wise to first view the directory and plan your visit. Try to avoid visiting the mall during rush hour. The area is heavily congested.

Tyson's Corner Mall
1961 Chain Bridge Road
McLean, VA 22102
703-893-9400
www.shoptysons.com

Naturally, one of the most premier shopping malls in the nation has a very fine play area. Tyson's Corner's National Geographic themed indoor play space is great for the five and under crowd. There's a pretend aboard recycling truck, little house with a small slide, beaver dam tunnel, and animals to climb on such as bees, polar bears, a turtle, and whales. The message of reduce, reuse, and recycle is embedded throughout. A bonus for some and a curse for others, there is a train ride (for a fee) that circles around the perimeter of the food court.

Insider Tip: The mall's "Kid Krusaders Kids' Club" offers almost weekly free entertainment, usually on Wednesdays and usually includes tunes by a local tot-rocker. Refer to the events page for information.

Chapter 7

Water Parks and Spraygrounds

Chapter 7: Water Parks And Spraygrounds

Drew Park
3514 22nd Street South
Arlington, VA 22204
703-228-6525
www.arlingtonva.us

This enclosed spray park is open from Memorial Day until Labor Day. There is also an on-site playground for children. Limited off-street parking is available. Restrooms are in the nearby community center. For current sprayground hours of operations check the website.

Fairfax Corner Fountain
4100 Monument Drive
Fairfax, VA 22030
703-222-4200
www.fairfaxcorner.com

Fairfax Corner is one of the most charming outdoor shopping centers in the area. The destination combines new architectural sensibilities with an old fashioned Main Street flavor. Along with a myriad of shops, restaurants and a movie theater is a lovely center square. When the weather turns warm, an interactive fountain rises from the ground and draws in children of all ages. The fountain is perfect for a summer day or ideal after some ice cream on a hot night. Restrooms are not available; however, there are a number of retail establishments you could duck into for a snack either before or after fountain time that have public restrooms. Be sure and bring a towel and sunscreen. While the fountain is wonderful, it is notorious for maintenance closures. Always check the website for hours of operations.

Great Waves Water Park
4001 Eisenhower Avenue
Alexandria VA 22304
703-960-0767
http://www.greatwaveswaterpark.com/

Located in Alexandria and run by the Northern Virginia Park Authority, Great Waves Water Park provides 20-acres of local family fun. An incredible wave pool, colorful intertwined tube slides, spray areas, a picnic pavilion and a large, outdoor seating area welcomes visitors. Little ones and parents can enjoy kid-friendly water slides and retreat to Minnow Bay for a swim. The park also features mini-golf, a batting cage and picnic shelters. The Riptide Cafe offers food. Bathrooms are available. Best to check the website for current hours of operation.

Hayes Park
1516 North Lincoln Street
Arlington, VA 22201
http://www.arlingtonva.us/

Hayes Park offers visitors a spray park as well as restrooms, water fountains, a playground and picnic shelter. The park is open from Memorial Day until Labor Day. Limited on-site and off-street parking. For current sprayground hours of operations check the website.

Lake Anne Park
11501 N. Shore Drive
Reston, VA 20190
www.reston.org

Set next to beautiful Lake Anne, this hidden gem offers a small spray park to escape to in the summer months. Visitors will also find basketball, tennis, and sand volleyball courts. There are restrooms, outdoor grills, a covered picnic area and 22 parking spots. If you are coming simply for the spray park and playground, this is one of the best for little ones. The destination is also ideal as a family picnic location.

Lyon Village Park
1800 North Highland Street
Arlington, VA 22201
www.arlingtonva.us

Safety conscious parents love this fenced-in spray park. The park is open from Memorial Day until Labor Day. In addition to the spray park, visitors will find a playground, picnic shelter and a large sandbox for little ones. There is limited off-street parking with varied hourly restrictions. Unfortunately restrooms are NOT available so plan accordingly. For current sprayground hours of operations check the website.

Our Special Harbor
6601 Telegraph Road
Franconia, VA 22310
703-922-9841
www.fairfaxcounty.gov/

Located in Lee District Park, this awesome sprayground opened in 2011 and is a local favorite due to its unique features and free admission. The sprayground includes a pirate ship, spraying dragon, small sprinklers, flowing water table play areas, and dumping buckets. Parents can expect to get wet along with their children. Water shoes are required to play. Bathroom and picnic facilities are available directly outside the sprayground. No food or drinks are permitted inside the water area.

Insider Tip: Although the facility is top-notch, it does not open until 11 a.m., which makes for a long morning for parents of early risers. Patrons start lining up early, and there is no shade in the line. If you can, go with a friend. One of you can wait in line while the other can watch the kids at the adjacent playground and give them a snack in the pavilion.

Powhatan Springs Park
6020 Wilson Boulevard
Arlington, VA 22205
703-228-PLAY
www.arlingtonva.us

Pirate's Cove
6501 Pohick Bay Drive
Lorton, VA 22079
703-339-6102
http://www.piratescovepohick.com/

See Chapter 2: Parks, Playgrounds and Marinas

Reston Town Center
11900 Market Street
Reston, VA 20190
www.restontowncenter.com

In addition to the scores of amazing shops, restaurants, theater and enchanting outdoor fountain, Reston Town Center now has an awesome spray park for kids! Tiered, shaded seating surrounds the spray park. It is perfect for overheated parents wanting to cool off whilst watching little ones. In the absence of designated restrooms, visitors typically use one of the numerous retail establishments at the Reston Town Center. Stop in for a snack and a bathroom break.

Insider Tip: Reston Town Center's pavilion is a wonderful venue that hosts live entertainment, kids' shows, a farmers' market in the warmer months and an outdoor ice skating rink in the winter.

Signal Bay Water Park
9300 Signal View Drive
Manassas, VA 20111
703-335-8872
www.manassasparkcommunitycenter.com

Located in the City of Manassas in Signal Hill Park, this water park boasts 27,000 sq. ft. of aquatic fun! Kids will love the lazy river, water cannons and slides. Parents and small children will appreciate the zero entry leisure pool with mushroom fountains. Signal Bay Water Park is open seasonally. A concession stand, picnic area, showers and restrooms are available. A playground is available in adjacent Signal Bay Park.

Splash Down Water Park
7500 Ben Lomond Park Drive
Manassas, VA 20109
703-361-4451
www.splashdownwaterpark.com

Splash Down is a local favorite for those that want a family-friendly water park sans the massive crowds that typically are found at larger parks. Kids and parents will enjoy the lazy river, endless assortment of slides, a leisure pool and the Big Kahuna Beach. A picnic pavilion, playground, sand volleyball court and tennis courts are also available. Splash Down Water Park offers birthday party packages that include: admission, a meal plan, a cake and staff assistance.

There are a number of food and refreshment options. The venue is stroller friendly. For those that may forget essentials like sunblock, there is a small on site gift shop. Restrooms and lockers are also available. Children of all ages are welcome. Admission fees are based on age and height.

Insider Tip: Splash Down Waterpark sits next to Ben Lomond Regional Park.

Upton Hill Waterpark
6060 Wilson Boulevard
Arlington, VA 22205
703-534-3437
http://www.nvrpa.org/park/upton_hill/

Nestled in Upton Hill Regional Park, Ocean Dunes Waterpark is a favorite destination for area residents. Children love the 500-gallon dumping bucket, water slides and fun waterfalls. Visitors can also take advantage of a generous pool that is perfect for family swimming and splashing. Ocean Dunes offers the Beach Break concession area and plenty of space for sunbathing or sitting on the surrounding deck area. Large play areas for smaller children, an impressive mini-golf course, batting cages and restrooms are also available.

Insider Tip: Ocean Dunes offers birthday parties packages and aquatic lessons.

Volcano Island Waterpark
47001 Fairway Drive
Sterling, VA 20165
703-430-7683
www.volcanoislandwaterpark.com

See Chapter 2: Parks, Playgrounds, and Marinas

Watermine Family Swimmin' Hole
1400 Lake Fairfax Drive
Reston, VA 20190
703-471-5415
www.fairfaxcounty.gov/parks/rec/watermine/

Run by the Fairfax County Park Authority, the Water Mine Family Swimmin' Hole has become a perennial favorite for local families and Fairfax County camps goers. Visitors will find an acre of sprays, flumes, water slides, showers, interactive play areas and a lazy river. There is a beach area for families as well as shade for those needing some relief from the sun. The venue is large enough to engage children of all ages but small enough for families to easily conquer it in a day. Restrooms are available on site. Arrive early to avoid the crowds. Large changing areas are available. Pizza is available or visitors can bring their own snacks and eat in designated areas. Younger children tend to enjoy the is destination more than older kids.

WaterWorks Waterpark
5301 Dale Boulevard
Dale City, VA 22193
703-680-7137
www.pwcparks.org

Located in Dale City WaterWorks is part of the Prince William County Parks & Recreation family. The large and inviting pool offers a number of fun slides, rope climbers, geysers and crayon sprayers. Little ones will enjoy the wading pool. WaterWorks has concession stands, shaded pavilions, a play area, coin operated lockers and restrooms. The venue offers season passes and birthday party packages. Visitors can find shaded spots to relax and the area is stroller friendly. WaterWorks is open seasonally from Memorial Day weekend until Labor Day weekend.

Chapter 8

Ice Skating and Roller Skating

Chapter 8: Ice Skating And Roller Skating

Outdoor Ice Skating in Northern Virginia

Harris Pavilion Ice Rink
9201 Center Street
Manassas, VA 20110
703-361-9800
www.harrispavilion.com

During the winter season, this public pavilion located in the cute City of Manassas contains a large outdoor skating rink. Skate rentals are available. The Harris Pavilion is next to the Manassas VRE Commuter rail line and is walking distance from many shops and restaurants. Check the website for designated free skating nights and special events.

Insider Tip: In the spring and summer, the ice rink goes away but the Harris Pavilion becomes home to free outdoor concerts and events. Many are family friendly.

Pentagon Row Ice Rink
1201 South Joyce Street
Arlington, VA 22202
703-418-6666
www.pentagonrowskating.com

Right in Pentagon Row in the middle of luxury shops and restaurants is a nice outdoor skating rink. Little ones can skate holding onto giant buckets for extra support. Fun music is always playing. Skate lessons, rentals, and birthday parties are also available.

Reston Town Center
11900 Market Street
Reston, VA 20190
703-709-6300
www.restontowncenter.com/pavilion.html

From early November through the second week in March Reston Town Center's outdoor Pavilion is transformed into a gleaming ice skating rink. Ice skates and other supplies are available inside the Skate Shop behind Clyde's. Every Friday Night enjoy a live DJ, games and prizes during Rock 'n' Skate. Every Saturday, kids can share the ice with the Cat in the Hat, Tweety Bird,

Scooby Doo and more favorite cartoon characters from 11:00 a.m. to 1:00 p.m. during the Saturday Morning Cartoon Skate.

Outdoor Ice Skating in DC

Georgetown Waterfront's Washington Harbor
3000-3050 K Street, NW
Washington, DC 20007
202-295-5007
www.thewashingtonharbour.com/Skating

This new 11,800 square-foot rink is the largest outdoor rink in DC and offers scenic skating alongside the Potomac River, public skating, lessons and exciting wintry fun through February.

National Gallery of Art Sculpture Garden
4th and Constitution Avenue NW
Washington, DC 20565
www.nga.gov/ginfo/skating.shtm

The National Gallery of Art Sculpture Garden Ice Rink is open mid-November through mid-March, weather permitting. View magnificent works of sculpture while skating in the open air and enjoying music from the state-of-the-art sound system. Rental skates and lockers are available. Food and drinks are available for purchase at the Pavilion Cafe.

National Zoo
2001 Connecticut Avenue, NW
Washington, DC 20008
www.nationalzoo.si.edu

During the winter, families can experience "iceless" skating at the Zoo's Picnic Pavilion on the world's best eco-friendly synthetic ice skating surface.

Indoor Ice Skating

Ashburn Ice House
21595 Smiths Switch Road
Ashburn, VA 20147
703-858-0300
www.ashburnice.pointstreaksites.com

The two NHL-sized ice rinks of the Ashburn Ice House host hockey leagues, figure skating, learn to skate lessons, birthday parties, camps and public skating. Fun Playground on the Ice programs for ages 8 and under includes bubbles, coloring, and snow. Pro-shop and skate rentals available.

Fairfax Ice Arena
3779 Pickett Road
Fairfax, VA 22031
703-323-1132
www.fairfaxicearena.com

Hockey, figure skating, learn to skate lessons, birthday parties, camps and public skating are available at this indoor rink in Fairfax. A pro shop, skate rentals, party rooms, skater's fitness room, and a cafe are also on site.

Hardcore Hockey
1800 Michael Faraday Court
Reston, VA 20190
703-709-1010
www.hardcorehockey.com

Hardcore Hockey provides an indoor rink for player/goalie lessons, camps and clinics. Contact venue for public skating hours and times. Skate rentals are available.

Haymarket IcePlex
15155 Washington Street
Haymarket, VA 20169
703-753-4423
www.haymarketiceplex.com

Haymarket IcePlex offers public skating, skating lessons, figure skating, ice hockey, and birthday parties. After collapsing under two feet of snow in 2010, the new and improved complex renovations include locker rooms, pro shop, snack bar, party rooms, heated viewing areas, and a hockey training area.

Kettler Capital Iceplex
627 N. Glebe Road
Arlington, VA 22203
703-243-8855
www.kettlercapitals.pointstreaksites.com/view/kettlercapitals

This state-of-the art iceplex with two indoor NHL-sized rinks is the official home of the Washington Capitals and offers public programs including lessons, hockey, skating, school break camps, and parties.

Mount Vernon RECenter Ice Arena
2017 Belleview Boulevard
Alexandria, VA 22307
703-768-3224
www.fairfaxcounty.gov/parks/rec/classes/ice.htm

This Fairfax County operated ice arena offers Hockey, figure skating, learn to skate lessons, camps and public skating, all conveniently located alongside the RECenter's fitness facilities and pool.

Prince William Ice Center
5180 Dale Boulevard
Woodbridge, VA 22193
703-730-8423
www.pwice.com

The Prince William Ice Center has it all: hockey, freestyle skating, parties, lessons, camps, public skating, pro shop, and a cafe.

Skatequest
1800 Michael Faraday Court
Reston, VA 20191
703-709-1010
www.skatequest.com

The modern and clean facilities at Skatequest include two indoor rinks open year-round for figure skating, ice hockey, lessons, birthdays, camps and public skating. Skate rentals, pro shop, and snack bar are also available.

Roller Skating

Bush Tabernacle Skating Rink
250 South Nursery Avenue
Purcellville, VA 20132
540-751-9806
www.bushtabernacle.com

This skating rink hosts open skate times, toddler skates, and also various teen center times with activities such as arcade games and sports. Inline and quad skates are available for rent in a variety of sizes, as well as adjustable skates for small children. Food and drinks are served daily.

Cavalier Family Skating
1924 Jefferson Davis Highway
Stafford, VA 22554
540-657-0758
www.cavalierfamilyskating.com

Cavalier Family Skating is a gigantic facility with roller-skating rentals, lessons, and birthday parties. There is also a playzone with large climbing structure with tunnels for children. Visit the website or call to find out about special discount times and events for families, such as the Disney Skate, where only Disney music is played.

Michael and Sons Sportsplex at Dulles (Dulles Sportsplex)
2160 Atlantic Boulevard
Sterling, VA 20166
www.dullessportsplex.com

A roller hockey league for children is available. See the website for registration information.

Skate-N-Fun Zone
7878 Sudley Road
Manassas, VA
703-361-7465
www.skatenfunzone.com

There are so many fun specials and events for families at Skate-N-Fun Zone. The venue rents and sells inline and quad skates. There is also a Laser Tag Arena for ages 4 and up as well as a large playzone, complete with a netted climbing structure. Skate-N-Fun Zone hosts birthday parties and gives skating lessons too.

Thomas Jefferson Center
3501 2nd Street South
Arlington, VA 22204
703-228-5920
www.arlingtonva.us

October-March, family and teen-only skating series are offered with a live DJ, moon bounces, and a cafe. Roller skating birthday parties are also available.

Vienna Community Center
120 Cherry Street, SE
Vienna, VA 22180
703-255-6360
www.viennava.gov

Family Skate Nights held in the Vienna Community Center gymnasium on Friday nights from January-March. Bring your own roller skates and safety equipment. Helmets are required. No scooters allowed. Parents are required to stay and are welcome to participate.

Chapter 9

Children's Theaters and Performances

Chapter 9: Children's Theaters & Performances

Alden Theatre
McLean Community Center
1234 Ingleside Avenue
McLean, VA 22101
703-790-0123
www.mcleancenter.org

Arts on the Horizon
1100 Wythe Street, #26093
Alexandria, VA 22313
703-967-0437
www.artsonthehorizon.org

Unique theater that offers performances as well as educational classes for little ones ages infant to 6 years of age. Performances are geared toward small children and their developing skills. Many of the shows can be seen at the Atlas Performing Arts Center in Washington DC.

Artisphere
1101 Wilson Boulevard
Arlington, VA 22209
703-875-1100
www.artisphere.com

Classika Theatre
2611 Jefferson Davis Highway, St. 103
Arlington, VA 22202
800-494-8497
www.classika.org

Creative Cauldron at ArtSpace Falls Church
410 South Maple Avenue
Falls Church, VA 22046
571-239-5288
www.creativecauldron.org

Dodgeball Theatre
1141 Elden Street
Herndon, VA 20170
www.dodgeballtheatre.com

Encore Stage and Studio
3700 Four Mile Run Drive
Arlington, VA 22206
(703) 548-1154
www.encorestageva.org

Started in 1967, Encore Stage & Studio is a unique venue that offers a number of annual theatrical productions. Different from other theaters, Encore Stage & Studio, under the guidance of theater professionals, allows young people the opportunity star and/or technically produce each show.

For budding thespians Encore Stage & Studio offers a number of workshops, theater classes and summer camps. Signers are encouraged to participate in the Encore Show Choir and Encore Traveling Theatre Club.

Hylton Performing Arts Center
10960 George Mason Circle
Manassas, VA 20109
703-993-7550
www.hyltoncenter.org

Hylton's 1,123-seat Merchant Hall is brilliantly designed to make every seat a good one. Free and easy parking, a soaring light-filled lobby, a friendly cafe, family-accessible restrooms, and world-class performers make Hylton a great choice for Northern Virginian families. Hylton's Family Series offer shows especially for children. In addition, regular shows that are designated "Family Friendly" offer 1/2-price discounts for children through grades 12 when accompanied by an adult.

Industrial Strength Theatre
Elden Street Player
269 Sunset Park Drive
Herndon, VA 20170
703-481-5930
http://www.eldenstreetplayers.org/

Jammin Java (Music)
231 Maple Avenue
Vienna, VA 22180
703-255-1566
www.jamminjava.com

Like most hidden gems in Northern VA, this unexpected surprise is found in a strip mall in Vienna. This musically inclined destination has broken through the glass ceiling of java house entertainment. Noted as one of the 5 best spots to see live music in the Metro DC Area, the location is daytime perfect for kids and a rare suburban treat for an adult evening with some of the area's best bands. The food, coffee and hour appropriate cocktails are wonderful.

During the week, the venue hosts all the most popular local children's performers such as Rocknoceros, The Great Zucchini, Oh Susannah and the grandsons Jr. Weekend shows often attract nationally known performers.

Mount Vernon Community Children's Theatre
1900 Elkin Street
Alexandria, VA 22308
703-360-0686
www.mvcct.com

Northern Virginia Players
Burke Community Church
9900 Old Keene Mill Road
Burke, VA 22015
703-866-3546
www.nvplayers.com

The Old Furniture Factory
6 W. Loudoun Street
Round Hill, VA, 20142
540-338-5050
www.theoldfurniturefactory.com

Pied Piper Theatre
9419 Battle Street
Manassas, VA 20110
703-330-ARTS
www.center-for-the-arts.org/piedpiper/

Housed in the Old Hopkins Candy Factory, the Pied Piper Theatre is a charming destination for local youth theater. Located in historic Old Town Manassas, the venue hosts three fully staged theatrical performances annually. The Pied Piper Theater also offers theatrical training and summers camps for ages 5 to adult.

Reston Center Stage
2310 Colts Neck Road
Reston, VA 20191
703-476-4500
www.restoncommunitycenter.com

Teens and Theatre Company
Arlington, VA 22203
703-371-7653
www.teensandtheatre.org

The Sterling Playmakers
P.O. Box 1611
Sterling, VA 20167
703-437-6117
www.sterlingplaymakers.com

Waddell Theater
1000 Harry Flood Byrd Hwy
Sterling, VA, 20164
703 450-2551
www.nvcc.edu

Located on the Northern Virginia Community College's Loudoun Campus, The Waddell Theater produces shows that invite student, faculty and local community members to participate in productions.

Wolf Trap - Children's Theater in the Woods
1551 Trap Road
Vienna, VA 22182
703-255-1900
www.wolftrap.org

This lovely outdoor theater in the woods plays host to a robust summer of live theater performance, Grammy winning musical groups, nationally renowned dance companies and more! Shows are hosted daily Tuesday through Saturday from late June until mid-August. While little ones are welcome, most shows are recommended for children ages 4 and up.

Chapter 10

Miniature Golf

Chapter 10: Miniature Golf

Algonkian Park
47001 Fairway Drive
Sterling, VA 20165
703-450-4655
www.nvrpa.org/park/algonkian

An inexpensive and newly re-designed mini-golf course that is fun and challenging for the whole family. The mini-golf course is fun to pair with the pool or Volcano Island Waterpark.

Broad Run Golf
10201 Golf Academy Drive
Bristow, VA 20136
703-365-2443
www.broadrungolf.com

Boasting a "play all day" rate with kids under three free, this golf course is open seasonally and contains fountains, bridges, rocks and more. Lighted for evening hours.

Burke Lake Park
7315 Ox Road
Fairfax Station, VA 22039
703-323-6601
www.fairfaxcounty.gov/parks/burkelakepark/

A basic but cute mini-golf course located near the popular Burke Lake train ride and ice cream parlor. Open seasonally. Check the website and Fairfax County Parktakes Magazine for coupons.

Cameron Run Regional Park
4001 Eisenhower Avenue
Alexandria, VA 22304
703-960-8719
www.nvrpa.org/park/cameron_run

This 18-hole mini-golf course contains covered bench areas to rest from the sun on a hot day. Cameron Run Park is also home to Great Waves waterpark and batting cages.

Dulles Golf Center & Sports Park
21593 Jesse Court
Dulles, VA 20166
703-404-8800
www.dullesgolfcenter.com

This world-class golf range also features mini-golf, beach volleyball, batting cages, the Chuck Will Golf Academy, and special event facilities.

(The) Dug Out & Islands in the Park
13241 Braddock Road
Clifton, VA 20124
703-818-3331
www.dugout-islands.com

Featuring "amenities only found in resort areas," Islands in the Park is beautifully landscaped with waterfall, streaming rivers, bridges, rock formations, and island holes. Also check out the batting cages at the adjacent "Dug Out" facility.

Fountainhead Regional Park
10875 Hampton Road
Fairfax Station, VA 22039
703-250-9124
www.nvrpa.org/park/fountainhead

The mini-golf course is a fun diversion when combined with the park's other amenities, such as boating, fishing, hiking, or mountain biking.

Jefferson Falls Mini-Golf
7900 Lee Highway
Falls Church, VA 22042
703-573-0444
www.fairfaxcounty.gov/parks/golf/jeffersongc/

Located next to a nine-hole executive golf course, this lighted mini-golf course is a fun option for locals.

Lake Accotink Park
7500 Accotink Park Road
Springfield, VA 22150
703-569-0285
www.fairfaxcounty.gov/parks/lake-accotink/

Despite being a small and basic mini-golf course this location offers tons of fun when combined with the nearby playground, boat rides, and carousel.

Oak Marr Mini Golf
3200 Jermantown Road
Oakton, VA 22124
703-281-6501
www.fairfaxcounty.gov/parks/golf/oakmarr/minigolf.htm

This traditional mini golf course is not elaborate, but is in a safe setting and is maintained well by Fairfax County. Restrooms and vending machines are available in the adjacent RECenter.

(The) Magic Putting Place
8902 Mathis Avenue
Manassas, VA 20110
703-257-PUTT
www.magicputtingplace.com

In addition to two separate 18-hole courses with a magic castle and fountain ponds, the Magic Putting Place features nighttime lighting, family friendly music, and a Snack Bar.

Pohick Bay Regional Park
6501 Pohick Bay Drive
Lorton, VA 22079
703-339-6104
www.nvrpa.org/park/pohick_bay

The Treasure Island mini-golf course is open May to October. Other park attractions include boating, camping, playgrounds, a water park, disk golf, and fishing.

Top Golf USA
6625 S. Van Dorn Street
Alexandria, VA 22315
703-924-2600
www.topgolf.com

This high-tech driving range includes 36 holes of mini-golf on Mountain and Valley Courses. Cocktails and a wide range of dining choices are available in the cafe.

Upton Regional Park
6060 Wilson Boulevard
Arlington, VA 22205
703-534-3437
www.nvrpa.org/park/upton_hill/content/miniature_golf

A small mini-golf course nestled in a popular urban park. Also check out Upton Regional Park for the playgrounds, Ocean Dunes Water Park, trails, and batting cages.

Woody's Golf Range
11801 Leesburg Pike
Herndon, VA 20170
703-430-8337
www.woodysgolf.com

In addition to one of the best themed miniature golf in the area, "Perils of the Lost Jungle", Woody's has something for everyone in the family including driving ranges, golf lessons, batting cages, volleyball, basketball, picnic areas, and birthday parties.

Chapter 11

Bowling

Chapter 11: Bowling

AMF Bowling Centers
www.amf.com/

AMF is the world's largest owner of bowling centers with Northern Virginia locations in Centreville, Annandale, Alexandria, and Woodbridge. In addition to bowling, AMF offer birthday parties, concessions and video arcade games.

Insider Tip: During the summer kids can register for free bowling all summer long as part of AMF's Summer Unplugged program. The Centreville location also offers a summer bowling clubs for kids in which kids meet weekly to bowl and receive bowling balls and character-themed T-shirts and prizes

Bowl America
www.bowl-america.com

Bowl America has multiple Northern Virginia locations in Manassas, Fairfax, Chantilly, Sterling, Falls Church, Alexandria, and Woodbridge. Bowl America locations offer parties, concessions and video arcade games.

Insider Tip: By enrolling in the Rolling Rewards program, students can earn free games of bowling.

King Pinz
1602 Village Market Boulevard
Leesburg, VA 20175
703-443-8001
www.kingpinzbowl.com

Although this local favorite features an upscale cigar bar, billiards, and sports grill, families are welcome throughout the day. Kids will love the Arcade and the futuristic glow-in-the-dark bowling lanes while parents will enjoy the restaurant-style dining, bar service, and plush couches.

Chapter 12

Paintball Parks and Laser Tag

Chapter 12: Paintball Parks and Laser Tag

Paintball Parks

Battlefield Paintball
16596 Greens Corner Road
Culpeper, VA 22701
540-829-6203
www.bfpaintballs.com

Hogback Mountain Paintball
20217 Hogback Mountain Road
Leesburg, VA 20175
703-777-0057
www.hogback.net

Pev's Paintball Park
39835 New Road
Aldie, VA 20105
703-327-7640
www.pevs.com

Powerline Paintball
2698 Poplar Road
Stafford, VA 22406
540-286-0404
www.powerlinepaintball.net

Skyline Paintball
363 Radio Station Road
Strasburg, VA 22657
540-465-9537
www.skylinepaintball.com

Laser Tag

Laser Nation
421 S. Sterling Blvd.
Sterling, VA 20164
703-450-2333
www.sterlinglasertag.com

Panther Family Laser Tag & Amusement Center
23520 Overland Drive
Sterling, VA 20166
703-661-4060
www.dulleslasertag.com

Shadowland Laser Adventure Center
5508 Franconia Road
Springfield, VA 22310
703-921-1004
www.shadowlandadventures.com

Skate-N-Fun Zone
7878 Sudley Road
Manassas, VA 20109
703-361-7465
www.skatenfunzone.com

Skyline Laser Tag
2012 S. Loudoun Street
Winchester, VA 22657
540-662-2272
www.skylinelasertag.com

UltraZone Laser Tag and Amusement Center
3447 Carlin Springs Road
Falls Church, VA 22041
703-578-6000
www.ultralasertag.com

Chapter 13

Arts & Crafts

Chapter 13: Arts & Crafts

art.smart.kids
Herndon and Reston VA
703-860-5820
www.artsmartkidsonline.com

Drop in for "ArtFul Afternoon" programs. The website has the most current information.

Creative Clay Studios
5704E General Washington Drive
Alexandria, VA 22312
www.creativeclaypottery.com

Drop in studio for creating pottery. Note, this is a place with pottery wheels and fire glazing to create vases, pots, and other pieces. It is not a paint-your-own pottery studio. This venue would be best with older children only. View the open studio times on the website.

Greater Reston Arts Center
12001 Market Street
Reston, VA 20190
703-471-9242
www.restonarts.org

Children can explore the galleries with a bucket of art supplies. See the museums and historical sites section for more information.

Michaels
Multiple Locations In Northern Virginia
www.michaels.com

Children can participate in arts and crafts classes, demos and events at Michaels locations throughout Northern Virginia. Passport to Imagination(TM) events are free and designed for ages 3 and up.

Thomas Jefferson Community Center
3501 2nd Street South
Arlington, VA 22204
703-228-5920
www.arlingtonva.us

Thomas Jefferson Community Center has drop in studio for photography, jewelry, pottery and woodshop for older children and teens. Experience is necessary since no instruction is provided. The Studios also host Girl Scout Workshops and the Paint-A-Plate program.

Chapter 14

Building Workshops

Chapter 14: Building Workshops

Build-A-Bear Workshop
www.buildabear.com

Visit the Fair Oaks and Potomac Mills Build-a-Bear locations to stuff, sew, personalize, and outfit your own cuddly friend.

Home Depot Kids Workshop
www.homedepot.com/

In addition to being the go to source for hardware, building, and garden supplies, Home Depot has free hands-on workshops the first Saturday of every month from 9:00 a.m. -12:00 p.m. Workshops are designed for children ages 5-12 and teach do-it-yourself skills, tool safety, and instill a sense of pride. Kids get to keep their craft and receive a free kids workshop apron, commemorative pin, and certificate of achievement.

Lego Store Mini-Builds
Tysons Corner and Potomac Mills
http://stores.lego.com/en-us/stores/us/tysons-corner/
www.stores.lego.com/en-us/stores/us/potmomac-mills-mall/

Visit the Tyson's Corner or Potomac Mills LEGO Store on the first Tuesday of every month and you can learn how to build a cool mini model, and take it home – for free! A new model will be available every month. Supplies are limited, so plan to arrive early and line-up for your free kit. Event is open to children ages 6 to 14 only.

Lowe's Build and Grow Clinic
Multiple Locations In Northern Virginia
www.lowesbuildandgrow.com

Lowe's Build and Grow Clinics are free to the public and occur every other Saturday at 10:00 a.m. See website for a list of scheduled clinics. Registration opens a few weeks before each clinic's date.

Sears Saturday Family Fun
Multiple Locations In Northern Virginia
www.sears.com/

Local Northern Virginia locations in Dulles Town Center, Falls Church, and Fair Oaks Shopping Center host Saturday kids' workshops. Kits usually cost $5.00 and can be purchased the day of the event. Space limited, R.S.V.P. with your local store online.

Chapter 15

Paint Your Own Pottery

Chapter 15: Paint Your Own Pottery

Art from the Heart
325 Garrisonville Road
Stafford, VA 22554
540-659-4092
www.yourartfromtheheart.com

Walk into this studio without an appointment to paint pottery, do glass fusing, and more. Parties are offered, as well as "Pottery to Go" kits. This allows customers to paint their pieces on their own time and bring it back to the studio for glazing. Refer to the website to learn about special events, such as creating keepsake ceramic pieces with a child's handprint/footprint or even a pet's pawprint too!

Clay Cafe Chantilly
13894 Metrotech Drive
Chantilly, VA 20151
703-817-1051
www.claycafechantilly.com

Consistently voted one of the best in the area, Clay Cafe Chantilly offers the largest selection of pottery and glass fusion pieces in the area. All materials are non-toxic, lead free, and safe for the environment. Besides pottery, artists can partake in orgami, bottle cap magnets, scrapbooking, beading, and card making. Always check the website for special events, coupons, and promotions. Birthday parties, scout programs, classes, and camps are also available.

Clay Cafe Falls Church
101 North Maple Avenue
Falls Church, VA 22046
703- 534-7600
www.claywire.com

This award-winning pottery and glass fusing studio is located in the heart of Falls Church and contains a large selection of materials and some of the best paint-your-own prices in the area. The website offers details about half-price nights, family packages, parties, events, and coupons. Please note, the space is very intimate, so it is best to call ahead to see if a party is scheduled before dropping by.

Color Me Mine Ashburn
22855 Brambleton Plaza
Ashburn, VA 20148
703-957-4020
www.ashburn.colormemine.com

This paint your own place in Brambleton offers a great selection of pottery and a great location near other shops and restaurants. All the paint used is non-toxic and safe for kids. Call ahead for the most current information.

Color Me Mine Fairfax
4209 Fairfax Corner Avenue
Fairfax, VA 22030
703-803-7246
www.fairfax.colormemine.com

So much of this paint your own pottery place is geared to kids. There are frequent kids' nights out and pajama paints on the calendar. Plus the studio has a fun location in Fairfax Corner that is close to shops and restaurants (as well as a summertime favorite, the Fairfax Corner Fountain.)

Paint This
1013 King Street
Alexandria, VA 22314
703-519-7499
www.paintthis.com

With a charming location in the heart of Old Town Alexandria, Paint This is a fun outing for kids of all ages. Select pottery products such as dinnerware, ceramic pieces, and picture frames, or try your hand at mosaics or glass fusion. Special group and party rates are available. Please check the website or call ahead for special events and promotions.

Paint Your Own Pottery
10417 Main Street
Fairfax, Virginia 2203
703 218-2881
www.ciao-susanna.com

Located right in the heart of Old Town Fairfax, Paint Your Own Pottery has a selection of over 600 pieces. Go in, select a piece, paint, and the staff will glaze and fire it within a few days. All of their glazes are also lead free and non-toxic. The latest hours, coupons, and updates are listed on the website. Also, make it a family date and take advantage of the great kid-friendly restaurants in Old Town Fairfax with great sandwiches at Panera Bread and Potbelly Sandwich Works. Or, for a full service meal, try the Greene Turtle or The Auld Shebeen.

Chapter 16

Jewelry Making

Chapter 16: Jewelry Making

Jewelry making is a fun activity at these local bead shops in NoVA. Most offer free studio time to put together your creation. Check the websites or call ahead for information about hours, the selection of beads, classes, events, and parties.

Bead Artist
521 F East Market Street
Leesburg, VA 20176
703-771-8115
www.beadartist.net

Beadazzled
Tysons Corner Center 1
1961 Chain Bridge Road
McLean, VA 22102
703-848-2323
www.beadazzled.net

Beads Limited
1801 Belle View Blvd
Alexandria, VA 22307
703-768-9499

Beads on Parade
10013 Jefferson Davis Highway Ste 105
Fredricksburg, VA 22407
540-710-0705
www.beadparade.com

Burke Gem and Beads
9415A Old Burke Lake Road
Burke, VA 22015
703- 425-3366
www.burkegemsbeads.com

Joy of Beading
5903 Lee Hwy
Arlington, VA 2220
703-532-3336
www.joyofbeading.com

Off the Beading Path
310 Mill Street Suite E
Occoquan, VA 22121
703-492-BEAD
www.offthebeadingpath.biz

Stars Beads
139 A Church Street, NW
Vienna, VA 22180
703-938-7018
www.starsbeads.com

The Potomac Bead Company
1104 King Street
Alexandria, VA 22314
703-299-8730
www.potomacbeads.com

Chapter 17

Sports Teams and Venues

Chapter 17: Sports Teams and Venues

Alexandria Aces
Frank Mann Field
3700 Commonwealth Avenue
Alexandria, VA 22205
www.alexandriaaces.org

This collegiate summer baseball club is part of the Cal Ripken League and welcomes spectators at Frank Mann Field in Alexandria. Food and concessions are available.

Michael & Sons Sportsplex At Dulles
2160 Atlantic Boulevard
Sterling, VA 20166
www.dullessportsplex.com

You will find 79,000-square feet of indoor sporting activities for leagues, camps, clinics and parties at Michael & Sons Sportsplex. Facilities include areas for hockey, lacrosse, soccer, skating, basketball, futsal and football.

Fairfax Sportsplex
6800 Commercial Drive
Springfield, VA 22151
www.fairfaxsportsplex.com

With over an acre of indoor fields, Fairfax Sportsplex is one of the area's largest indoor sports venues providing indoor soccer, volleyball, youth clinics, and tot soccer programs. The Fairfax Sportsplex features a large observation deck and snack bar, locker rooms, and state-of-the art lighting and floor surfaces.

George Mason University
Patriot Center
4500 Patriot Center
Fairfax, VA 22030
703-993-3000
www.gomason.com

Every year the Patriot Center plays host to a lively season of George Mason Sports such as Men's and Women's Basketball. With easy access, ample parking, reasonably priced tickets and great seats, this local venue makes for an easy and fun family outing. The Patriot Center is located in the heart of the City of Fairfax on the campus of George Mason University.

Haymarket Senators
John Champe High School
41535 Sacred Mountain Street
Aldie, VA 20105
www.eteamz.com/haymarketbaseball

Haymarket Sportsplex
6614 James Madison Highway
Haymarket, VA 20169
www.haymarketsportsplex.com

Kettler Capitals Iceplex
627 N. Glebe Road
Arlington, VA 22203
571-224-0555
www.capitals.nhl.com

The Kettler Capitals Iceplex serves as the training facility and home to the National Hockey League's Washington Capitals' offices. Check the website for schedule of practices that are open to the public free of charge.

NoVA Roller Derby
Game Played @ Dulles Sports Complex
21610 Atlantic Boulevard
Sterling, VA, 20166
www.novarollerderby.com
703-430-9966

Don't let the gruff exterior fool you, the ladies of the NoVA Roller Derby play with heart both on and off the rink. Started in April 2011, the NoVA Roller Derby league has married a passion for flat track roller derby with a commitment to helping local charities. The ladies of the league are all volunteers that dedicate measurable time, energy and talent to putting on a show for fans that also benefit local organizations such as women's shelters, animal rescue leagues and military families to name a few. Derby events are held at Dulles Sports Complex. Tickets are reasonably priced and children under 6 get in for free. These are family-friendly events. Many of the participants are local moms who are out there to have a little fun while helping neighbors. Food, drink and restrooms are available on-site. Spectators need to bring their own chairs. Check the website for upcoming bouts and charitable events.

Potomac Nationals
7 County Complex Court
Woodbridge, VA 22192
703-590-2311
http://www.milb.com/

The Potomac Nationals is the perfect local baseball fix for parents and children. Save yourself the trip into Washington DC and keep some money in your pocket. The Potomac Nationals are a minor league affiliate team of the Washington Nationals. The team plays at Pfitzner Stadium located in Woodbridge, VA. The stadium has become a hometown favorite for locals. Expect to find reasonable prices, great seats and a fun kid's club loaded with perks. The park also offers a great birthday party package for kids.

Insider Tip: The July 4th game offers a great night of food, fireworks and fun! Plus, there are fireworks on many weekend nights throughout the whole summer.

Potomack Lakes Sportsplex
20280 Cascades Parkway
Sterling, VA 20165
703-444-1459
www.loudoun.gov

Potomack Lakes Sportsplex is a 47-acre athletic complex with four lighted softball fields, six soccer fields, large playground, pavilion, meeting room, and concession stand with rest room facilities. The complex hosts up to 29 tournaments per year and has won numerous National awards. Pavilion next to the playground is available for a rental fee.

Washington Redskins Training Camp
21300 Redskins Park Drive
Ashburn, VA 20147
703-726-7411
www.redskins.com
www.redskinskidsclub.com

Fans can register online to attend Washington Redskins practices and Fan Appreciation Day at the Redskin training camp in Ashburn. There is no guarantee, but always a possibility that coaches and players will sign autographs for fans after practice. Kids Club Members can get VIP tent access on a first-come, first-served basis.

Insider Tip: Don't forget to bring your free online camp fan invitation. Invitations will be collected at the front gate. Bring your own chairs or blanket and arrive early to get a good position around the practice fields. Parking is free. Snacks and beverages available for purchase in CASH only. Souvenirs are available for purchase with cash or credit card. Fans are allowed to bring their own food and non-alcoholic beverages. Photography is permitted, but no video cameras are allowed.

Chapter 18

Skateparks

Chapter 18: Skateparks

Alexandria Skatepark
3540 Wheeler Avenue
Alexandria, VA 22066
703-838-4343
www.alexandriava.gov/Recreation

Birchdale Recreation Center
14730 Birchdale Avenue
Dale City, VA 22193
703-670-9118
www.pwcparks.org

Catoctin Skatepark
141 Catoctin Circle, SE
Leesburg, VA 20175
703-777-8837
www.leesburgva.gov

Costello Skatepark
99 Adams Street
Manassas Park, VA 20111
703-335-8872
www.cityofmanassaspark.us

Old Town Manassas Skatepark
9005 Tudor Lane
Manassas, VA 20110
www.manassascity.org

Powhatan Springs Park
6020 Wilson Boulevard
Arlington, VA 22205
703-228-PLAY
www.arlingtonva.us

Skate Park on Wheels
Vienna, VA
703-255-5721
www.viennava.gov

Van Dyck Park
3730 Old Lee Highway
Fairfax, VA 20004
www.fairfaxva.gov/parksrec/parkrule.asp - SP

Veterans Memorial Regional Park
14300 Featherstone Road
Woodbridge, VA 22191
703-491-2183
www.pwcparks.org/

Wakefield Skate Park
8100 Braddock Road
Annandale, VA
703-321-7081
www.fairfaxcounty.gov/parks/skatepark/

Chapter 19

Campgrounds

Chapter 19: Campgrounds

Whether your family is camping for the first time or wants to stay close to home, Northern Virginia offers some great camping options.

Blue Ridge Regional Park
Bluemont, VA 20135
703-352-5900
www.nvrpa.org/

Enjoy tent camping in a beautiful setting in the Blue Ridge Mountains for organized youth groups only.

Bull Run Regional Park
7700 Bull Run Drive
Centreville, VA 20121
703-631-0550
www.nvrpa.org/

Camp here with your family at one of the tent, RV sites, or rustic cabins. Full service sites available. Open year round.

Burke Lake
7315 Ox Road
Fairfax Station, VA 22039
703-323-6600
http://www.fairfaxcounty.gov/parks/burkelakepark/

Campsites are open April to October for RV and tent camping.

Cedar Mountain Campground
20114 Camp Road
Culpeper, VA 22701
540-547-3374
www.cedarmtn.com

Located on a lake setting with tent and RV camping sites.

Lake Fairfax
1400 Lake Fairfax Drive
Reston, Virginia 22039
703-471-5415
www.fairfaxcounty.gov/parks/lakefairfax/fairfaxcamp/

Open year round, tent and RV campsites.

Pohick Bay Regional Park
6501 Pohick Bay Drive
Lorton, VA 22079
703-339-6104
www.nvrpa.org/park/pohick_bay/content/camping

Enjoy Pohick Bay by staying at a tent, RV site, or one of the park's rustic cabins. The park offers great amenities, including a one-mile loop that connects the campground to Gunston Hall.

Prince William Forest
18170 Park Entrance Road
Triangle, Virginia 22172
703- 221-7181
www.nps.gov/prwi/planyourvisit/camping.htm

The largest campground in Northern Virginia, Prince William Forest has three front country campgrounds, one backcountry campground, and five cabin camps.

Shenandoah National Park Camping
Multiple Sites in Shenandoah National Park
www.nps.gov/shen/planyourvisit/camping.htm

Not too far from the DC Metro is one of the most beautiful national parks in the country, Shenandoah National Park. There are many camping options as well as other accommodations. It's a great destination for a long weekend!

Chapter 20

Amusement Parks

Chapter 20: Amusement Parks

Busch Gardens & Water Country USA
1 Busch Gardens Boulevard
Williamsburg, VA 23187
800-343-7946
http://seaworldparks.com/en/buschgardens-williamsburg

For those that don't want to make the trip to Disney World, Busch Gardens is a lovely and more manageable alternative. The European-themed adventure park offers visitors 100-acres of state-of-the-art rides and rollercoaster including the Verbolten, Mach Tower℠ and Griffon. Young children will enjoy the Sesame Street Forest of Fun play area as well as many kid-friendly attractions and rides.

When its time for a break you'll find a wide range of culinary treats from the different countries represented in the park including: England, France, Germany, Ireland and Italy. During the summer months you can extend your stay and take in nearby Water Country USA, Colonial Williamsburg or Virginia Beach. In the fall enjoy special Halloween and Oktoberfest events. In winter, the park twinkles with millions of lights during the popular Christmas Town celebration including holiday shows, sleigh rides, visits to Santa's workshop, and the parks' 50-foot tall, light-animated Christmas tree.

Insider Tip: Look for special discounts and membership passes on the website including free seasonal passes for Virginia resident preschoolers.

Great Wolf Lodge Waterpark
549 E. Rochambeau Drive
Williamsburg VA 23188
757-229-9700
www.greatwolf.com/williamsburg

Even when the weather outside is frightening, the whole family will enjoy Great Wolf Lodge's 84-degree indoor water park with over 79,000 square feet of water fun for everyone including slides for thrill seekers and splash pools for little ones. Spend the night and families can rest up for the next day in camp-themed rooms with separate miniature tents and log cabins for the kids. Great Wolf Lodge is a fun destination in itself but is also convenient as a home base for visiting other Williamsburg attractions.

Paramount's Kings Dominion
16000 Theme Park Way
Doswell, VA 23047
804-876-5000
www.kingsdominion.com

Kings Dominion is one of the closest large-scale theme parks in the area. It rests 75 miles south of Washington DC. Little ones will enjoy a number of kid-friendly rides as well as the Snoopy's Starlight Spectacular, a fun light show. Thrill seekers will love the WindSeeker, a 301-foot-tall tower swing ride. Older children will go wild for Dinosaurs Alive!, an animatronic dinosaur park that features 40 life-sized, roaring, moving dinosaurs. Children 3 and older require an admission ticket. Ride height guidelines are listed, by ride, on the website. There is on-site lodging and camping as well as local hotels to choose from. Summer visitors can visit WaterWorks. Experience rushing rivers, a 650,000-gallon wave pool, a lazy river and water slides. Entrance is free with park admission to Kings Dominion.

Insider Tip: Visitors can get deeper discounts by purchasing tickets online prior to a visit. Military families get a discount.

Chapter 21

Parent Support Groups

Chapter 21: Parent Support Groups

DC Metro Dads
www.dcmetrodads.com

DCMetroDads supports stay-at-home and primary caregiver fathers. Membership is extended to fathers living in the DC Metro area. Playgroups, educational activities, DADS Nights Out and outings to popular local venues are offered to members.

DC Working Moms
www.dcworkingmoms.com

DC Working Moms supports working mothers through an active online forum and occasional lunch and evening events. The group has membership throughout Northern Virginia. Membership fees may apply.

Holistic Moms Support Group
www.holisticmoms.org

The Holistic Moms Network connects parents who are interested in holistic health and green living. Most groups hold monthly meetings. Some chapters host guest speakers and offer playgroups, mom's night out events and book clubs. The group strives to generate national awareness, education and support for holistic parenting. Currently there are support groups in Alexandria, Arlington, Burke, Fairfax and Springfield. Membership fees are required.

MOM's Club International
www.momsclub.org

This group caters to stay-at-home-moms and offers a number of local groups including: Alexandria, Annandale, Arlington, Ashburn, Bristow, Falls Church, Fairfax County, Springfield and more. They offer a number of outings and activities for mother and child. MOM's Club International focuses on support for the mother. Children are taken care of by other mommy volunteers while women meet to discuss the challenges and needs of stay-at-home-moms. Membership fees are required.

Mothers First
www.mothersfirst.org

Mother's First focuses on the support of stay-at-home-moms through a social network that meets regularly. Groups can be found in Burke/Fairfax, Chantilly/Centreville, Great Falls, Reston/Herndon, and Vienna/McLean. Membership fees are required.

Mothers of North Arlington
www.monamoms.org

This organization serves stay-at-moms, mothers who work part-time and mothers with home-based businesses. The diverse Arlington, VA based organization has a strong network that includes activities, varied support groups and even a babysitting coop. Membership fees are required.

Mothers & More - Northern Virginia Chapters
www.mothersandmore.org

Mothers & More supports stay-at-home and working mothers. Mothers & More offers a number of educational classes for members. Mothers can connect online and in person. Check the website to connect with a local chapter. Membership fees are required.

Newcomers & Moms Clubs Worldwide Directory
www.newcomersclub.com

The Newcomers & Moms Clubs is an umbrella site for many organizations. The directory is meant to provide end users with a list of possible organizations and groups that might assist them in creating friendships in a new area. Membership fees may apply.

Vienna Moms Inc.
www.viennamoms.org

Serving Vienna and Oakton, VA, Vienna Moms caters to stay-at-home moms and those moms working part time. The group has an assortment of activities including daytime playgroups with children of similar ages, children events as well as mom's night out events. The group also has a strong forum that can provide with an endless list of local, trusted vendors in the DC Metro area. Membership fees are required.

MOPS (Mother of Preschoolers)
www.mops.org

MOPS is internationally known and trusted mothers' group. The MOPS organization supports every mother with a child from conception to kindergarten. There are a number of local chapters that meet regularly as well as a strong virtual community. Check the website to find your local chapter. Membership fees apply.

Parent's Groups For Multiples:

Eastern Prince William Mothers of Multiples
www.bigtent.com/groups/epwmomclub

Membership is open to mothers and expectant mothers of multiples. Member benefits include: monthly meeting, an online community, mom's night out events and a consignment sale. Membership fees apply.

Fairfax County Mothers of Multiples
www.fcmom.org

Fairfax County Mothers of Multiples Club is a support group for mothers, grandmothers, legal guardians, and expectant or adoptive mothers of twins, triplets, and beyond. They currently have chapters in Alexandria, Burke, Centreville, Falls Church, Herndon, Fairfax, McLean, Springfield, Oakton, Reston, Vienna, Stafford and Woodbridge. The organization provides events and activities including: playgroups, family activities, mom's night, a semi-annual consignment sale and monthly meetings. Membership fees apply.

Loudoun/Fairfax Mothers of Multiples Club
www.lfmomc.net

This group supports parents and grandparents of multiples in Loudoun County and parts of Fairfax County. Membership provides organized playgroups, interactive member message board, monthly meetings, a semi-annual consignment sale, kid-friendly events and membership to the National Organization of Mothers of Twins Club (NOMTC). Membership fees apply.

Northern Virginia Parents of Multiples
www.nvpom.com

This group supports parents, grandparents and legal guardians of multiples throughout Northern VA. Membership provides organized playgroups, an online community, monthly meetings with featured speakers, a semi-annual consignment sale, kid-friendly activities and parent's night out activities. Membership fees apply.

Prince William County Mothers of Multiples
www.pwmomc.org

Provides support for parents of multiples in Eastern and Western Prince William County, Loudoun and Fauquier County. Membership provides: organized playgroups, monthly meeting, guest speakers, seasonal outings and celebrations and a semi-annual consignment sale. Membership fees apply.

Chapter 22

Childcare Support

Chapter 22: Childcare Support

ASAP Sitters

www.asapsitters.com

This local agency provides babysitting referrals throughout Northern Virginia.

Let Mommy Sleep

www.letmommysleep.com

The only baby nurse agency that serves the DC Metro, Northern Virginia, and Baltimore area. Overnight newborn care and sleep consultations.

Meghan Leahy Parent Coach

www.positivelyparenting.com

Personal and group parent coaching on topics such as power struggles, parent relationships, and child behavior.

Parenting Playgroups

www.parentingplaygroups.com

Dr. Rene Hackney offers parenting classes on a variety of subjects such as potty training and positive discipline. Social skills groups are also available.

Sleepwell Sleep Solutions

www.sleepwellsleepsolutions.com

Sleepwell provides gentle sleep coach and green-proofing services.

Chapter 23

Parenting Publications

Chapter 23: Parenting Publications

Kid Trips Northern Virginia Edition
(eBook, Online and Print resource)
www.GoKidTrips.com

You've got the book, now stay connected by signing up for our free blog and newsletter at www.GoKidTrips.com. You can also get updates, seasonal event information, and travel tips on http://www.facebook.com/GoKidTrips and www.twitter.com/GoKidTrips.

Northern Virginia Magazine
(Print and Online resource)
www.northernvirginiamag.com

The online section of Northern Virginia Magazine has a family feature section with articles about local events and personalities. Subscribe to their family newsletter for more updates, product reviews, and suggested outings.

NoVA Outdoors
(Online resource)
www.novaoutdoors.com

NoVA Outdoors is the premier playground review website in the area. Find reviews with photographs of hundreds of local parks and playgrounds in Arlington, Alexandria, Fairfax, Fauquier, Loudoun, Prince William, and some more rural counties too.

Our-Kids
(Online resource)
www.our-kids.com

Our-Kids is the greater D.C. metro area's most comprehensive online family website. The members' area boasts a database of over 800 events per week. Events can be sorted by age, price, event type, and location. Members also receive a jam-packed weekly newsletter and access to giveaways and contests.

Washington FAMILY Magazine
(Print and Online resource)
www.washingtonfamily.com

Washington FAMILY Magazine is a regional parenting publication that includes interest articles, an event calendar, and resource pages. The magazine is free and distributed at nearly 3,000 locations in the D.C. Metro area. Sign up for their weekly email newsletter and follow them on Facebook for the latest updates.

Washington Parent Magazine
(Print and Online resource)
www.washingtonparent.com

Washington Parent Magazine is a monthly, free magazine that features articles by local experts, a monthly calendar, and annual guides. Each month has a different theme for the annual guide. Past guides have included camps, childcare, and children's wellness. The magazine is free and available at many local libraries and grocery stores.

Chapter 24

Seasonal Fun

Chapter 24: Seasonal Fun

January

Chinese Lunar New Year Parade
www.chineseparadedc.com

Starting the day of the Lunar New Year (which usually falls late January or early February) and including the ten days following, there are celebrations, fireworks, restaurant specials, and cultural performances hosted by Chinese cultural associations throughout the DC area. Drawing over 40,000 spectators, the most popular local event is the Chinese New Year Parade in DC's Chinatown. With dragon dances, music, and colorful displays, this is a fun celebration for the entire family, but the streets can get crowded so plan travel accordingly. The closest metro station is Gallery Place/Chinatown and a good place to view the Parade is along 7th Street between G Streets and I.

Chinese New Year Festival
www.chinesenewyearfestival.org

Celebrate the Chinese New Year at Luther Jackson Middle School in Falls Church with live music, Asian dancers, children's games and crafts, Asian cuisine, cooking demonstrations, Chinese language workshops, and the popular dragon parade.

Lunar New Year Celebration
www.shopfairoaksmall.com

Special Asian exhibitions, performances, children's craft workshops, and ceremonies are held each year during this two day celebration in Fair Oaks Mall Grand Court including dragon dances, martial arts demonstrations, and a lantern festival.

Martin Luther King, Jr. Day

With the 2011 dedication of the impressive Martin Luther King, Jr. Memorial near the site of the civil rights leader's famous "I Have A Dream" speech, Washington DC has an important role in honoring Dr. King's legacy. The third Monday in January the city hosts numerous commemorations, readings, theatrical productions and concerts. The Martin Luther King, Jr. Memorial, District of Columbia's Martin Luther King Jr. Memorial Library, and the Smithsonian Museum of American History host many of these events.

In Northern Virginia, annual events include Reston Community Orchestra's Martin Luther King, Jr. Tribute, Arlington's Martin Luther King, Jr. Tribute at Washington-Lee High School, and the Martin Luther King, Jr. Day Celebration at McLean's Alden Theatre. In addition, people across the country can come together by registering or participating in a local community service project as part of the Martin Luther King Jr. Day of Service.

Sugarloaf Craft Festival
www.sugarloafcrafts.com

World-class crafters gather at the Dulles Expo Center to show their wares in a lively atmosphere with live entertainment, special children's performances, and plenty of food.

Presidential Inauguration & Parade
www.inaugural.senate.gov

Every four years on January 20, DC pulls out all the stops to celebrate Inauguration Day. But attending a fancy Inaugural Ball or gala isn't the only way to celebrate a new Presidential term. Anyone can witness the Swearing-in-Ceremony and Inaugural Address on large screens set up along the National Mall. During the ceremony and Inaugural Address these crowds have been known to stretch down the entire Mall. [In spite of frigid temperatures, the 2009 Inauguration of Barack H. Obama drew an estimated 1.8 million people, the largest attendance of any event in the history of Washington, DC.]

Families can also enjoy the Inaugural Parade and may even get a glimpse of the First Family as they travel by motorcade down Pennsylvania Avenue along with inaugural floats, citizens groups, color guards, and marching bands. Want to avoid the crowds? Check the schedule for the full dress rehearsal held a week or so before the Inauguration along the parade route.

A word about security: If you plan to attend any of the Inaugural events or even travel within the vicinity, be prepared for long lines at security checkpoints and be aware that there is a long list of items that are specifically prohibited within designated security perimeters (including backpacks, coolers, thermoses, strollers, umbrellas, duffel bags, tripods, camera bags, and more). Special events may also be planned throughout the week, so be prepared for road closures and extra security all week long.

Washington Auto Show
www.washingtonautoshow.com

This annual auto show provides some welcome indoor fun in January. In addition to shopping for your next dream car, there is a terrific area for kids where they can meet favorite characters and enjoy family-friendly entertainment and activities. The best part, tickets for children under 5 are free.

Washington Nationals Natsfest
http://washington.nationals.mlb.com/index.jsp?c_id=was

Show your team spirit for the Washington Nationals Major League Baseball Team by joining in this annual fan festival at the Washington Convention Center.

February

Alexandria's George Washington Birthday Celebration and Parade
www.visitalexandriava.com
www.washingtonbirthday.org

In addition to the country's biggest parade celebrating our First President, Alexandria's citywide George Washington Birthday Celebration includes a 10k race, a Birth night Banquet and Ball, and free admission in many of the city's historic sites.

Black History Month

In Northern Virginia, visitors can walk in the footsteps of African-Americans escaping slavery at The Underground Railroad event at Leesylvania State Park , visit Alexandria's Black History Museum, or learn about life as a slave at Mount Vernon. Over the river in DC, Black History month is celebrated with a month of special programming, theatrical performances, concerts, and family-friendly activities at venues including the National Portrait Gallery, District of Columbia's Martin Luther King Jr. Memorial Library, the African American Civil War Memorial and Museum, the U.S. Navy Memorial, the Frederick Douglass House (whose birthday is celebrated February 12), the Anacostia Community Museum, Mary McLeod Bethune Council House, Arlington House, and the Martin Luther King Jr. Memorial Library.

Discover Engineering Family Day
www.nbm.org

This popular and free program at the National Building Museum event offers kids the chance to build, learn, explore and invent. Favorite PBS characters are known to make special appearances.

George Washington's Birthday Celebration at Mount Vernon
www.mountvernon.org

Mount Vernon celebrates our first President's birthday with free admission all day, a wreath-laying ceremony, patriotic music, military performances on the Bowling Green, and appearances by "General Washington" himself.

Museum Month

During the month of February, museums across the country offer special tours, film series, events, and admission specials. Check www.culturaltourismdc.com for a round up of special museum events planned in DC.

March

Adventures in Travel Expo
www.adventureexpo.com

Take a vicarious vacation by exploring a wide variety of adventure travel packages and tours. Kids will love the fun-filled demonstrations and activities like rock-climbing, performances, and hands on activities such as animal encounters. Travel celebrities such as Rick Steves, Andrew Zimmerman, and Arthur Frommer often make guest appearances.

Chocolate Lovers Festival
www.chocolatefestival.net

This two-day festival in the City of Fairfax is held the first full weekend in March. Among the delicious events planned each year are the Taste of Chocolate, an arts extravaganza where the medium is chocolate, a pancake breakfast featuring chocolate chip pancakes, children's activities, open houses at historic buildings, and more. Some events require a fee, but many are free to all visitors.

DC's St. Patrick's Day Parade
http://dcstpatsparade.com/

Don yourself in green and get ready for a parade filled with floats, marching bands, Irish Dance troupes, and bagpipers. The parade is typically held from noon to 3:00 p.m. the Sunday before St. Patrick's Day and travels along Constitution Avenue between 7th and 17th Streets. Grandstand tickets are available, but standing along the route is free.

Gunston Hall Kite Festival
www.gunstonhall.org

Come fly a kite in the pastures of historic Gunston Hall during what is considered to be one of the area's finest family events. Children can also play 18th-century games, see period puppet shows, sample hearth cooking, and climb on a fire truck. Bring a picnic or buy one there.

National Capital Boat Show
www.gsevents.com

The annual boat show at the Dulles Expo Center is the largest in the area. Children will enjoy climbing on the boats and pretending to drive. Adults dream of life as a lottery winner!

National Cherry Blossom Festival
www.nationalcherryblossomfestival.org

For the Metro DC area this event is a spring right of passage. The three-week celebration celebrates the 1912 gift of 3,000 cherry trees by the city of Tokyo with cultural performances, food, festivals and a parade. It is truly breathtaking to see the trees in bloom along the Jefferson Memorial & Tidal Basin. Parking is tight along the Tidal Basin, so plan to arrive at the crack of dawn, bike, walk, or take the Metro.

National Shamrock Festival
www.shamrockfest.com

DC turns green for the weekend with a gigantic festival at RFK stadium. Enjoy live entertainment, booths, carnival rides, games, Irish history, culture, and of course plenty of Guinness.

Old Town Alexandria's St. Patrick's Day Celebration & Parade
www.ballyshaners.org

Old Town's St. Patrick's Day Celebration is a family favorite that includes a fun dog show in Market Square, a classic car competition along King Street, and a terrific parade beginning at King and West Streets. Due to the popularity of this event, traffic can get gridlocked, so it's best to come early, take public transportation or walk to the festivities.

Ringling Bros. and Barnum & Bailey Circus
www.ringling.com

When the circus comes to town, the elephants parade past the Capitol towards the Verizon Center. Performances are held at the Verizon Center in DC and the Patriot Center in Fairfax traditionally the end of March and beginning of April.

Smithsonian Kite Festival
www.nationalcherryblossomfestival.org

Bring your own kite or just come and behold the spectacle as kite flyers from across the country flock to the National Mall to compete for prizes. Special demonstrations and kite making workshops are available for children as well. The event is held as part of the Cherry Blossom Festival. Information about the rules and registration can be found on the festival's website.

Ticonderoga Spring Festival
www.ticonderoga.com

Open on weekends from March-April (depending on where Easter falls), this festival offers all the regular family fun activities of Ticonderoga as well as some special Easter and springtime fun.

April

DC International Film Festival
www.filmfestdc.org

This growing annual film festival brings more than 100 outstanding films from over 55 countries to venues across DC. Film programming consists of fiction, documentaries, animation, and terrific programs for families and kids.

Earth Day
www.earthday.org/mall

Celebrate Earth Day on the National Mall with live entertainment, interactive exhibits, renewable energy demonstrations, and embassy and non profit booths. The event is free and open to the public. Earth Day events and volunteer projects are also hosted in Fairfax County, Prince William County, Arlington, Alexandria, and Loudoun.

White House Easter Egg Roll
www.whitehouse.gov/eastereggroll

A major event in the metro area, the iconic national event includes egg coloring, art activities, face painting, music, magicians, and of course an egg hunt. Tickets are required to attend. The National Park Service holds an online lottery about a month prior to the event.

Leesburg Flower and Garden Festival
www.leesburgva.gov

Over 150 vendors offer the best in landscape designs, gardening ideas, supplies and tools, flowers, herbs, plants, outdoor living items, and more. There are plenty of activities for children including entertainment, crafts, interactive displays, and lots of food vendors.

Fairfax Spotlight on the Arts Festival
www.visitfairfax.com

Fairfax Spotlight on the Arts is an annual three-week festival that showcases area visual and performing artists at various venues in and around the City of Fairfax.

National Zoo African-American Family Day
www.nationalzoo.si.edu

This annual festival of Easter Egg hunts, storytelling, art, and music is held every Easter Monday at the National Zoo.

National Park Week
www.nps.gov/history/parkweek

For a week in April, typically the third week, enjoy free admission, junior ranger programs, and special events at all National Parks.

Sakura Matsuri Japanese Street Festival
www.sakuramatsuri.org

This huge cultural festival in DC offers live music, dances, activities, a marketplace, and Japanese food.

Shakespeare's Birthday Celebration
www.folger.edu

The Bard's birthday is celebrated with cake, costumed characters, and fun activities for the whole family at The Folger Shakespeare Library.

Smithsonian Craft Festival
www.smithsoniancraftshow.org

This annual festival of fine American crafts is held every year in the National Building Museum. Admission for children under 12 is free.

Thomas Jefferson's Birthday
www.nps.gov/thje

On April 13, the Jefferson Memorial celebrates the birthday of Thomas Jefferson with a wreath laying, speeches, and a military ceremony.

USA Science & Engineering Festival
www.usasciencefestival.org

A gigantic festival held over two days at the Washington Convention Center, there are thousands of booths, interactive exhibits, amazing inventions, entertainment for all ages, and celebrity appearances. Because of the gigantic size and amount to see, it is impossible to get to everything this festival has to offer. It is highly recommended to plan out your day ahead of time by using the schedules and map available on the website. The next scheduled festival is in 2014.

Washington Nationals Home Opener
http://washington.nationals.mlb.com/index.jsp?c_id=was

The Washington Nationals kick off the baseball season in April with fun activities for the family including the Running of the Presidents. Kids will also enjoy the Family Fun Area with play equipment, batting and pitchers cages, and more. Check the website for special promotions for kids and families, including membership in the MVP Nats Kids Club.

May

Andrews Air Force Base Annual Air Show
www.jsoh.org

Every May, thousands of fans stream onto Andrews Air Force Base for the popular joint services air show featuring parachute jumps, aerial feats, and the Blue Angels. There is plenty on the ground to enjoy too, including aircraft tours, military vehicles, exhibits, moon bounces, ride simulators, and more. Spectators are required to take the Branch Avenue Metro or park at FedEx Field and take a shuttle bus to the base. Plan to arrive first thing in the morning to beat the lines for the shuttles. Collapsible strollers, baby formula and diaper bags are allowed, but backpacks, outside food and beverages are not. Please carefully review security instructions in advance and pack accordingly. Mom-recommended items to bring: lawn chairs or a blanket (much of the viewing area is concrete), earphones or earplugs, hand-wipes (for clean-up after the port-o-potties), hats, sunglasses and plenty of sunscreen!

Cinco De Mayo Festival
www.marumontero.com

Thousands of people converge on the National Mall for the annual Cinco De Mayo Festival. Enjoy a full day of music, dance, food and even a children's pavilion. Children can learn how to make piñatas, weave strands of colored yarn into decorative braids, and decorate beautiful fans.

City of Falls Church Civil War Day
www.fallschurchva.gov

This living-history event depicts the Falls Church home front during the Civil War. Activities include drilling and firing demonstrations, living history presentations, a Civil War music concert, and free admission to the Cherry Hill Farmhouse.

Claude Moore Colonial Farm 1771 Market Fair
www.1771.org

Held on the third full weekend of May, July, and October, the 18th Century Colonial Market Fair offers a chance to eat and drink, play games, enjoy a puppet theatre, watch craftsmen at work, and enjoy tales from costumed interpreters on this working historical farm in McLean.

Delaplane Strawberry Festival

www.delaplanestrawberryfestival.com

This local favorite is held every year at Sky Meadows State Park over Memorial Day Weekend. Families can enjoy hayrides, live entertainment, 4H petting zoo, pony rides, 5K fun run, field games for all ages, local crafters, and, of course, delicious fair food including funnel cake, crab cakes, strawberry shortcake and more. Flats of fresh strawberries are available to take home.

Dragon Boat Festival

In addition to watching the dragon boat races on the Potomac River, families can enjoy performances, food, and hands on activities that celebrate Chinese culture. Check the web for more information

Herndon Festival

www.herndonfestival.net

Usually held the last weekend in May, this popular annual event attracts over 80,000 people from all over the metro area. Featured events include live entertainment, international foods, carnival rides and games, children's entertainment, free children's hands on art activities, 10K & 5K races, model railway exhibit, and an arts & crafts show. Admission is free.

Loudoun County Spring Farm Tour

www.loudounfarms.org

For two weekends in May, many of Loudoun County's breathtaking farms and vineyards are open to the public with demonstrations and special events. Refer to the Loudoun County Farm Tour website for participating farms and directions.

McLean Day

www.mcleancenter.org

The whole town comes together to celebrate in Lewisville Park with booths, entertainment, food, games, and carnival rides.

Memorial Day Festival and Parade - City of Falls Church
www.fallschurchva.gov

Veterans ceremony, 3K Fun Run, live entertainment, contests, food and craft vendors, and a nostalgic old-time parade down Park Avenue with fire trucks, bagpipes, and local marching bands.

Memorial Day Parades and Concerts – DC
www.nationalmemorialdayparade.com

Patriotic floats, marching bands and veterans from all 50 states converge on DC to honor the men and women who have served in our Nation's military. The parade starts in front of the Capitol and moves down Constitution Avenue towards the White House. Wreath-laying ceremonies are held at the Tomb of the Unknown Soldier in Arlington National Cemetery, the Vietnam Veterans Memorial, and the U.S. Navy Memorial. The National Symphony Orchestra also holds a free concert on the West Lawn of the Capitol featuring famous performers. In addition to the official commemorations, as part of an annual pilgrimage known as Rolling Thunder, over 500,000 war veterans and supporters ride their motorcycles to the Nation's Capital in support of veteran, POW and MIA groups. Kids love to watch as Rolling Thunder blazes a trail through the DC area on their way to the Pentagon and memorials.

National Cathedral Flower Mart
www.nationalcathedral.org

This two-day flower festival is held outdoors on the beautiful Cathedral grounds. You will find music and entertainment along with more than 50 boutique booths, filled with gifts for the home and garden. Ride the antique carousel, which is only open for this event. Flower Mart features plant sales, floral and horticultural displays, boutique booths, tasty foods, and fun activities for children. Usually held the first weekend in May.

National Train Day Events
www.nationaltrainday.com

Celebrate National Train Day by searching for events in the DC, VA, and MD area.

Northern Virginia Fine Arts Festival
www.northernvirginiafineartsfestival.org

Held mid-May in Reston Town Center, this festival features hundreds of outstanding artists, musical entertainment, interactive performances, hands-on exhibits, and a popular children's art tent.

Passport DC International Children's Festival
www.culturaltourismdc.org

Throughout the month of May more than fifty embassies open their doors to visitors to share their cultures and customs.

Spring Farm Day at Frying Pan Park
www.fairfaxcounty.gov/parks/fryingpanpark

Visit with baby animals, watch sheep shearing demos, enjoy games, wagon rides, and more at Fairfax County's favorite kid-friendly farm.

Sunset Celebration at Mount Vernon
www.mountvernon.org

Held Memorial Day weekend, visitors have the opportunity to take evening tours of the mansion, sample food, participate in 18th century games, dancing, and wagon rides.

Taste of Arlington in Ballston
www.tasteofarlington.com

This annual street festival includes live entertainment, children's activities, and delicious bites from local restaurants. Drawing an average of 15,000 people each year, this event fills the streets of Ballston with tons of fun.

Virginia Gold Cup
www.vagoldcup.com

For over 80 years, Virginia's Gold Cup has been celebrated as the crown jewel of steeplechase. You will find everything from the hats and pearls crowd to normal folks that are just there to take in the sites and sounds of Gold Cup. Regardless of your social standing, this is a fun day at the races for all. Lots of food, fun and plenty of spirits are the backdrop of this local favorite. The event is typically held the first Saturday in May.

Virginia Renaissance Festival
www.varf.org

Held May-June at Lake Anna Winery, the festival boasts lots of costumed entertainment, demonstrations, shopping, children's activities, and of course lots of food. This is definitely the place to chomp on a giant turkey leg.

Viva Vienna
www.vivavienna.org

Viva Vienna is a community festival held on Memorial Day weekend with crafts, vendors, entertainment, and amusement rides.

June

Asian Food and Tennis Festival
www.asianfestivaldc.com

This unique cultural festival showcases tennis, music, live performances and Asian food at George Mason University.

Artomatic
www.artomatic.org

This is the area's biggest creative arts festival with visual art, music, fashion, film, performance, photography and more. This event takes place on the weekends in June in Crystal City, Arlington. Taking the metro is recommended.

Celebrate Fairfax! Festival
www.celebratefairfax.com

This huge 3-day festival is held every June at the Fairfax County Government Center and is Northern Virginia's largest community-wide celebration. The 25-acre site is filled with 300 exhibitors, food vendors, crafters, carnival rides, live concerts on eight stages, children's activities, a petting zoo, karaoke competition, and a Inova's Train Ride to Good Health. Highlights including nightly fireworks and national headline performers draw crowds in the tens of thousands.

DC Jazz Festival
www.dcjazzfest.org

Jazz performances are featured at more than 40 venues over 10 days in June and also include Family Fun days.

Manassas Heritage Railway Festival
www.visitmanassas.org

Little engineers will love the model train displays, live music, train memorabilia, and more. Train excursion rides to Clifton and back occur throughout the day.

Manassas Wine and Jazz Festival
http://www.visitmanassas.org/

This popular Father's Day event includes wine tasting and entertainment.

National Capital BBQ Battle
www.bbqdc.com

This spicy cook-off along Pennsylvania Avenue features tastings from great BBQ restaurants, cooking demonstrations, and special children's activities and entertainment.

Northern Virginia Summer Brewfest
www.novabrewfest.com/

In late June, many of America best breweries come together in Leesburg for beer tasting, great food, and entertainment. Children are admitted free and most of the events in the Family Fun area are also free.

Smithsonian Folklife Festival
www.festival.si.edu

Held over several weekends in June and July, this huge festival stretches down the National Mall and showcases different cultures and themes each year. Families can enjoy plenty of international food, crafts, and activities. Although food must be purchased, admission, entertainment, and activities are free.

Taste of Reston
www.restontaste.com

Spotlighting the many restaurants and cuisines offered in Reston, VA, this festival also has lots of entertainment, a family fun zone, and hands on kids cooking activities.

Washington Folk Festival
www.glenechopark.org

This is a free festival that showcases music, dance, performers, and craftspeople in the greater Washington DC area. Usually held the first weekend of June.

Wolf Trap's Children's Theatre-in-the-Woods
www.wolftrap.org

From late June through August, this outdoor theatre in Wolf Trap has weekly musical performers, puppet shows, and plays for children. Nationally renowned acts are often featured.

July

Alexandria Waterfront Festival
www.waterfrontfestival.org

Just a few days after the Nation's Birthday, Alexandria celebrates the event along with its own birthday on July 7 with a free concert by the Alexandria Symphony Orchestra, birthday cake, food and fireworks at Oronoco Bay Park. This event is free.

4th of July on the National Mall

The mack daddy of all annual DC events is the celebrated 4th of July festivities on the National Mall replete with celebrity bands, fireworks and a big old parade. This is one that you have to get to at least once in your life. Yes, the crowds can be a bit much but if you go early and use Metro you will be in good shape. The parade kicks off at 7th & Constitution. The event culminates with fireworks that are set off around 9 p.m. Most agree this is a LONG day and best meant for older kids. Infants and toddlers tend to poop out in the sun, heat and extended hours.

Best places to view the DC fireworks from Virginia's shores include the Marine Corps War Memorial, the Air Force Memorial, and Long Bridge Park. However, there are plenty of localities in Virginia that host their own parades, fireworks, and celebrations at venues that are far more kid-friendly and accessible.

An American Celebration at Mount Vernon
www.mountvernon.org

This annual 18th-century style celebration on July 4th includes fireworks, a naturalization ceremony, patriotic music, old-fashioned fun and activities, and visits by "George and Martha Washington."

Celebrate America in Old Town Manassas
www.visitmanassas.org

This all-American party in Old Town Manassas boasts one of the largest Fourth of July fireworks displays in Northern Virginia. Leading up to the fireworks, the streets surrounding the Old Town train depot, the Harris Pavilion and the Manassas Museum are filled with rides for the kids, live entertainment, concessions, and a red, white, and blue hayride.

Loudoun County Fair
www.loudouncountyfair.com

This is a massive county fair with a carnival, bull riding, dairy show, horsemanship, pet shows, obstacle course, children's activities, live music and more.

August

Arlington County Fair
www.arlingtoncountyfair.us

A fun event that is filled with competitive exhibits, farm animals, food, community vendors, carnival games and rides, and live entertainment. This is a big fair and very stroller friendly too.

Brick Fair
www.brickfair.com

Brick Fair brings together LEGO fans for two days of fun at the Dulles Expo Center every August with LEGO models, displays, vendors, friendly competitions and plenty of hands on games and activities for adults and children alike.

Dog Days Peach Festival
www.greatcountryfarms.com

In addition to plenty of u-pick peaches in Great Country Farms' orchards, this fun event for families and canines features an impressive agility course, retriever contests, Doggie Olympics and performances. All visiting dogs should be on a leash and be wearing a valid rabies certification tag. Families may also visit the Country Store, Roosteraunt, and giant five-acre play area.

Fairfax County 4-H Fair and Farm Show
www.4hfairfax.org

Held annually at Frying Pan Farm Park, the fair includes farming demonstrations, horse shows, 4-H Exhibits, dog shows, farm animals, live entertainment, antique tractor pulls, and carnival rides. Each year the festival keeps getting bigger and better. Come early to avoid the crowds.

Friendship Firehouse Festival
www.alexandriava.gov

The Friendship Veterans Fire Engine Association holds its annual Firehouse Festival each year on the first Saturday in August. The popular family event features antique fire equipment, craft booths, displays by Alexandria merchants, and live entertainment.

Flying Circus Annual Hot Air Balloon Festival
www.flyingcircusairshow.com

This high-flying annual event features hot air balloon launches, parachute jumpers, wing walkers, and feats by barnstormers in vintage biplanes.

Lucketts Fair
www.theluckettsfair.com

Over 100 crafters, antiques vendors, music, demonstrations, contests, and great food including BBQ, country ham, and Luckett's famous hand-churned ice-cream. For the kids: pony rides through the woods, farmyard petting zoo, and old-fashioned hay rides.

Prince William County Fair
www.pwcfair.com

A highly regarded county fair with animals, midway exhibits, carnival rides, local vendors, food, interactive booths and more. Visit the website for information about special discount days and coupons.

Shakespeare Free For All
www.shakespearetheatre.org

A Washington DC tradition which offers free performances at the Shakespeare Theatre to the public in the late summertime. Tickets can be gained in an online lottery or at a designated location the day of the performance.

Virginia Scottish Games
www.vascottishgames.org

Enjoy being a spectator for athletic events, bagpipe shows, a British car and bike show, fiddling dancing, and even a dog show. Besides the competition there are specialty vendors, craftspeople, and British/Irish food specialties.

Washington Redskins Training Camp
21300 Redskins Park Drive
Ashburn, VA 20147
703-726-7411
www.redskins.com
www.redskinskidsclub.com

Training camps are held in July or August. Visitors are encouraged to bring chairs or blankets. The practices last around two hours, and fans may get autographs afterwards. Free admission.

September

Alexandria King Street Art Festival
www.visitalexandriava.com

Old Town's King Street becomes an open-air gallery of more than 200-juried artists. Families will especially enjoy the interactive activities at the Torpedo Factory Art Center. Free.

Black Family Reunion
www.ncnw.org/events/reunion.htm

The Black Family Reunion Celebration is a cultural event that attracts more than 500,000 people each year. The 3-day festival focuses on health, education and economic empowerment in the African American community. The celebration includes a VIP Gala, themed pavilions and an enchanting evening R&B concert on the National Mall. The event is held in early September.

Bluemont Fair
www.visitloudoun.org

Nestled in the foothills of the Blue Ridge Mountains, this authentic county fair in the historic village of Bluemont offers live music, 10K race, juried crafters, artisan demonstrations, antiques, local art, wine tastings, pie and pickling contests and more. Kids will enjoy the children's fair, pony rides, and caboose. This event is usually held the second week in September.

Colonial Market and Fair at Mount Vernon
www.mountvernon.org

This annual event is free with regular Mt. Vernon admission. Colonial dressed artisans demonstrate and sell their crafts. Families can participate in 18th century games and watch Revolutionary War drills. Even George and Martha wander around for the merriment. During this weekend only, Potomac River sightseeing cruises are free of charge.

DC Green Festival
www.greenfestivals.org

This nationwide events heads to the DC Convention Center at the end of September and offers entertaining and enriching activities for families include eco-crafts, yoga, story time and more. By visiting the Green Kids Zone families can learn about protecting and conserving water, eco-systems, animal species and habitats.

Fall for Fairfax Festival
www.fallforfairfax.com

An annual, free festival at the Fairfax County Government center with vendors, rides, petting zoos, food, entertainment, big trucks, and fall activities.

Fairfax Fall for the Book Festival
www.fallforthebook.org

A weeklong festival with readings and lectures by nationally acclaimed authors.

Fall Festival and Taste of Falls Church
www.fallschurchva.gov

Held each September in Cherry Hill Park, this festival includes live entertainment, pony rides, amusement rides, crafters, children's activity tent, and food from Falls Church restaurants.

Herndon Labor Day Festival
www.herndon-va.gov

Children can enjoy free admission and kids' activities. Adults can sample wines and microbrews, eat gourmet foods, and visit with upscale craft vendors.

KORUS Festival at Bull Run
www.koreancelebration.com

KORUS is a large three-day event in Bull Run Regional Park that is dedicated to Korean culture, food, and entertainment.

Mount Vernon Colonial Market and Fair
www.mountvernon.org

Dozens of America's finest craftspeople will be on hand to demonstrate their 18th-century crafts and sell their traditional wares. The event also features 18th-century music, fire-eating, sword-swallowing, puppet and magic shoes, and hearty food. This weekend only, you can also take a free sightseeing cruise from the dock.

National Book Festival
www.loc.gov/bookfest

The festival is free and open to the public and features more than 70 award-winning authors, illustrators and poets appearing in "Fiction & Fantasy," "Mysteries & Thrillers," "History & Biography," "Children," "Teens & Children," "Poetry," and "Home & Family" pavilions. Activities for children, which are fun and promote reading, can be found in the popular "Let's Read America" pavilion. Check out the Library of Congress WW I pavilion. The Pavilion of the States brings representatives from throughout the country to the festival with information on local reading and literacy programs. This is a great day and message for children. This event is held in late September.

National Symphony Orchestra Labor Day Concert
www.kennedy-center.org/nso/

Take a moment to soak in the official last moments of the summer at The National Symphony Orchestra free Labor Day Weekend concert. Held on the West Lawn of the U. S. Capitol, the annual concert is led by the NSO Associate Conductor. This fun event is family friendly. The Kennedy Center lists concert information under its "Performance Calendar" tab. The concert is typically held the Sunday of Labor Day Weekend at 8 p.m.

Virginia Indian Festival
http://www.fairfaxcounty.gov/parks/riverbend

Spend the day at Riverbend Park meeting Native Americans from different tribes, see dance performances, try throwing a spear or shooting a bow, shop for Native American crafts and jewelry, and learn about early Indian life.

October

Air & Scare at the Steven F. Udvar-Hazy Center
www.airandspace.si.edu/airandscare

This is a safe, indoor trick or treating for kids at one of the area's most popular museums. Mars sponsors the event and the candy is plentiful. There are spooky-crafts, science demonstrations, and Halloween themed activities. This is an extremely well attended event and so it is best arrive early!

Annual Alexandria Art Safari
www.torpedofactory.org

This free day of hands-on-arts and crafts activities for kids and their families is a great way to explore new materials and techniques. Artists also hold demonstrations where children are able to work with artists' tools themselves or learn about an art form by watching and interacting with the artist.

Boo at the Zoo
www.nationalzoo.si.edu

This Halloween favorite has been attracting little ghosts and goblins for years. Harry Potter, Dora the Explorer and even Spiderman can be seen at this fun, festive annual event at the National Zoo in Washington DC for kids ages 2 to 12. Costumed volunteers hand out candy, snack food and special treats at 40+ treat stations. Animal encounters, zookeeper chats, Halloween decorations and zoo animals will be on hand for the fun!

Burke Nursery and Garden Center Fall Festival and Pumpkin Playground
www.pumpkinplayground.com

The Burke pumpkin playground is a local favorite with a fun hayride, plenty of climbing structures, slides, and bales of hay to climb on. Burke is smaller than some of the other pumpkin playgrounds but still has plenty to do and is an especially good pick when you'd rather do more playing and less walking. Everyone gets a free pumpkin when they leave.

Centreville Day
www.centrevilleva.org

Centreville Day is held at the Historic Centreville Park and includes free children's rides and activities, living history and tours, live entertainment, local food vendors, and an open-air marketplace.

Claude Moore Farm Autumn Colonial Market Fair
www.1771.org

Market Fair entertainers, tradesmen and militiamen will be on hand for demonstrations and entertainment. Have your fortune told or purchase a charm from the Gypsy Fortune Teller. Kids will enjoy learning to dip a candle or turn a piece of wood on the carpenter's lathe. Holiday crafts, period food, beverages and wares are available for purchase.

Clifton Day
www.cliftonday.com

Held on the Sunday before Columbus Day, this annual festival includes arts and crafts, antiques, demonstrations, the Town Market, live music, children's activities and local food vendors. For added fun, ride the train from Burke (Rolling Road) or from Manassas.

Corn Maze in the Plains
www.cornmazeintheplains.com

Corn mazes, pumpkins, farm animals, and hayrides are all part of the fall fun at the Corn Maze in the Plains. Moon Light Maze from 6-10:00 p.m. on Fridays and Saturdays.

Cox Farms Fall Festival
www.coxfarms.com

This is the Northern Virginia's largest fall festival and is an annual tradition for many families. The awesome festival offers up hayrides, pumpkin tosses, kid-friendly farm animals, giant slides, rope swings, live entertainment, a playground for preschoolers, kettle corn, and apple cider. Bring a sturdy stroller since the ground can get muddy.

Del Ray's Art on the Avenue
www.artontheavenue.org

This annual street festival on Mount Vernon Avenue features 300-juried artists, three stages with live music, hands-on art activities for kids, and local food specialties.

Del Ray Halloween Parade
www.visitdelray.com

Thousands of costumed pets, strollers, children and adults show off their creativity as they parade down Mt. Vernon Avenue and end in the athletic fields next to the Mount Vernon Recreation Center. Awards are given for best pet costume, best decorated business, best decorated home and best decorated stroller.

Falls Church Halloween Carnival
www.fallschurchva.gov

This Falls Church event invites infants through sixth graders to come in costume and enjoy carnival games, a moon bounce, face painting, crafts, a haunted house, movies, candy, and a creepy creature show at the Falls Church Community Center.

Fall Harvest Family Days at Mount Vernon
http://www.mountvernon.org

Fun during Fall Harvest Family Days at Mount Vernon includes wagon rides, wheat treading in the 16-sided barn, 18th-century dancing demonstrations, a straw bale maze, blacksmithing demonstrations, apple-roasting, corn husk dolls demonstrations and early-American games and music.

Falloween at the Market Common Clarendon
www.marketcommonclarendon.net

Kids will love this annual event with a petting zoo, face painting, sidewalk chalking, live entertainment, plus trick-or-treating at participating retailers. People and pets in costume are invited to join in the FALLoween Parade. Each attendee can also take a complimentary mini-pumpkin home. No registration necessary and all the activities are free.

Farm Day
www.fallschurchva.gov

Farm Day is held every October in Cherry Hill Park in the City of Falls Church. This family event features horse-drawn hayrides, pumpkin painting, scarecrow making, a petting zoo, tours of the Cherry Hill Farmhouse, and farming demonstrations. Children can also learn farming skills such as apple butter making and corn-shelling.

Fire Prevention Week
www.firepreventionweek.org

Many fire stations across the nation open their doors to the public this week (usually the second week in October) to educate children about fire safety. Contact your local fire station for possible open house hours. Activities vary by station and may include tours, rescue demonstrations, fire hose games, suiting up in a fireman's equipment, and climbing in a fire truck.

Great Country Farms Fall Festival and Pumpkin Glow Night
www.greatcountryfarms.com

The highlight of this month long fall festival is Glow Night, when over 1500 carved jack-o-lanterns are lit and displayed in the fields. Families can also enjoy a bonfire, roasting marshmallows, pumpkin carving competitions, and picking the perfect pumpkin.

Hallowmarine at the National Aquarium
www.aqua.org

Put on your costume and make the trip to Baltimore for creepy-crawly critter encounters, Halloween activities, a scavenger hunt, and more at the National Aquarium. Hallowmarine activities are included in the price of admission. To guarantee your tickets, purchase them online ahead of time.

Kids Euro Festival
www.kidseurofestival.org

A month long celebration of free performances, workshops, and events at venues in the DC, Maryland, and Northern Virginia area.

Leesburg Animal Park's Pumpkinville
www.pumpkinfestleesburg.com

In addition to visiting the animals, during Pumpkinville, visitors to Leesburg Animal Park can enjoy hayrides, pony rides, giant hill slides, kids hay maze, straw tunnels, rope swings, moon bounces, all you can eat apples, fresh cider, pumpkin patch, scarecrow decorating, and a kids playground area. Extra activities on the weekends include a zip-line, mini tractor rides, camel rides, and live entertainment.

Long Branch Hot Air Balloon, Wine & Music Festival
www.historiclongbranch.com/balloonfestival.htm

Held against the backdrop of the scenic Blue Ridge Mountains, the fields of Long Branch are filled with all the colors of the rainbow when these majestic hot air balloons rise into the sky. The event also features children's activities, entertainment, crafts, antique fire trucks and, of course, wine.

Marine Corp Marathon
www.marinemarathon.com

The Marine Corp Marathon is the 4th largest US Marathon and 7th largest in the world. One of the most memorable moments for those that finish the MCM is what happens after you pass the finish line. Runners receive their official finisher's medal from the men and women of the Marine Corps. Kids can get in on the action with the Healthy Kids Fun Run and the Finish Festival.

Manassas Fall Jubilee
www.visitmanassas.org

Enjoy live entertainment, rides, a farmer's market, pumpkin patch, vendors, and family activities at this festival in historic Old Town Manassas

Oktoberfest Reston
www.oktoberfestreston.com

This popular festival at the Reston Town Center features a carnival, live entertainment, fall brews, and traditional Oktoberfest fare from area restaurants.

Shenandoah Valley Hot Air Balloon & Wine Festival
http://www.historiclongbranch.com

The Shenandoah Valley Hot Air Balloon & Wine Festival is a fabulous 3-day annual event. The quaint town of Longbranch plays host to this charming festival, held every October. Stunning fall foliage and the intoxicating Blue Ridge Mountains make up the backdrop for the festival. The majestic sky is filled with hot air balloons throughout the event. The festival also features a huge array of children's activities, entertainment, artisans & crafters, antique fire trucks and more! The venue is 60 miles from Washington D.C. Once simply a Hot Air Balloon Festival, it has expanded to the Shenandoah Valley Hot Air Balloon, Wine and Music Festival.

Temple Hall Fall Festival and Corn Maze
www.nvrpa.org/park/the_maize

In addition to a pick-your-own pumpkin patch, this Loudoun County festival has some wild and crazy fun including pumpkin blasters, massive pillow jumping, paintball shooting gallery, and a pig race.

Ticonderoga Farms Fall Festival
www.ticonderoga.com

Ticonderoga Fall Festival attractions include hayrides, pick-your-own pumpkin, playground, hayrides, slides, tunnels, antique fire trucks, Virginia's longest swinging bridge, panda puzzle bamboo maze, petting farm animals, and an Indian Tee Pee Village. On the weekends, the Cow Pow train and Enormous Jump & Bounce Pillow are also operational.

Washington International Horse Show
www.wihs.org

One wouldn't expect to see so many amazing horses and equestrians in downtown DC, but this annual Verizon Center event will surprise and delight horse lovers of all ages. Notable: there is a Kids' Day on Saturday during which families can learn about horses, take a pony ride, meet some horses up close, and participate in free activities.

November

Bull Run Festival of Lights
www.nvrpa.org/park/bull_run_festival_of_lights

This is a NoVA holiday favorite event. Drive through and check out the impressive animated light displays that are timed to music in the comfort of your own vehicle. Always check online for coupons. A carnival is available on the weekends, but please note that weekdays are much less crowded. It runs from mid-November through early January.

Belvoir Officer's Spouse Club Craft Boutique
www.belvoirosc.org

Housed in the George Mason University field house, this event boasts hundreds of vendors, children's activities, food, and entertainment. Lots of handmade and unique gifts are for sale.

Busch Garden's Christmas Town
www.buschgardens.com

Opening on Black Friday, Christmas Town has become a magical family tradition offering world-class entertainment, many of Busch Garden's regular rides, and a Santa's Workshop area. The park is decorated completely with beautiful lights and decor, and families can have a truly unforgettable holiday outing.

City of Fairfax Annual Holiday Craft Show
www.fairfaxva.gov/

What started out as a small craft show has now become a premium arts and crafts festival with artisans from all over the United States. Held annually at Fairfax High School, this weekend show is a wonderful opportunity to find unique holiday gifts.

ICE! - Christmas at the Gaylord National Resort
www.gaylordhotels.com

Open from November through the first week in January, this annual display of colorful ice sculptures and ice slides features different Dreamworks character themes each year. Additional activities, such as gingerbread decorating, a train ride, visits with Santa, a scavenger hunt, and beautiful musical fountain light show are available inside the Gaylord National Resort.

Joyful Noise Bazaar
www.joyfulnoisebazaar.com

Enjoy free admission and shop at upscale vendors and artisans. There are gourmet sweets, children's activities, and live entertainment too.

Manassas Veterans Day Parade
www.manassasveteransparade.org

This is the largest Veteran's Day parade in the Washington DC area. Parade includes military units, bands, various vehicles, and pipe and drum teams.

Meadowlark Gardens Winter Walk of Lights
www.nvrpa.org/park/winter_walk_lights

Experience over 500,000 LED lights and amazing displays at Meadowlark Botanical Gardens as you walk through this magical display. Enjoy hot chocolate or roast s'mores in the fire pit. Online coupons and deals are often available.

Northern Virginia Christmas Market
www.dullesexpo.com/

This market is a giant local craft and artisan event where shoppers can find unique gifts. Kids under twelve are admitted free.

Reston Town Center Holiday Parade
www.restontowncenter.com/holidays/parade.html

Enjoy Macy's-style balloons and amazing floats at this festive parade held on the Friday after Thanksgiving. Families will love the antique cars, marching bands, dancers, community groups, and of course the stars of the show--Santa and Mrs. Claus!

December

Christmas at Mount Vernon
www.mountvernon.org

On selected days and evenings from the last week in November through the first week in January, families can get in the holiday spirit by learning about the Washington's' Christmas traditions, meeting historical characters, touring the mansion by candlelight, and singing carols in front of a bonfire.

First Noon, First Night, And New Year Celebrations

The biggest New Year's Celebration in Northern Virginia is First Night Alexandria. Tickets are required, but with the annual Fun Hunt, 90 live performances, children's activities, and a spectacular finale at midnight, it is well worth the price of admission. Another popular family event is the City of Falls Church Watch Night. This annual, free New Year's Eve celebration is typically held from 7 p.m. to midnight near the crossroads of Broad and Washington Streets in Falls Church. Children's entertainment includes magicians, storytelling, face painting, and a moon bounce.

In Vienna, families can have a kiddie rockin' good time at Jammin' Java's annual Rocknoceros New Years Eve Party. At press time, the popular annual First Night Leesburg had been cancelled, but locals are hopeful that the downtown tradition will resume in the future.

If you are willing to drive across the river to National Harbor, a terrific new tradition has been started with the National Children's Museum Noontime New

Year's. If you have the stamina to stay through the night, the National Harbor New Year's Celebration caps off the night with fireworks.

Gunston Hall Plantation Christmas
www.gunstonhall.org

Costumed characters will greet your family at this enchanting annual Christmas event at Gunston Hall. Ride in a horse-drawn carriage, sip warm cider by the fire, and sample period food prepared in the hearth kitchen. A wonderful way to experience the Christmas season as it was in the 18th century. This one-day event includes a 30-minute mansion tour in the price of admission and does not require reservations.

Holiday Parade of Boats
www.visitalexandriava.com

At dusk more than 50 illuminated boats cruise the river at Old Town Alexandria's waterfront. Festivities begin in the afternoon at Alexandria City Marina behind the Torpedo Factory.

Holiday Sing-Along at Wolf Trap
www.wolf-trap.org

While this is a free event, it is recommend to arrive early to secure seating. Throughout this popular annual Marine Band concert, the audience is invited to sing along with holiday, Christmas, and Hanukkah songs. Don't forget to bring a toy for the Toys for Tots collection!

Leesburg Holiday Parade and Festival
www.idalee.org/

A fun community parade with floats, trucks, performers, music, Santa, and more. Festival and additional performances follow the parade.

Lighting of the National Menorah
www.afldc.org

Music, children's activities, latkes and doughnuts follow the annual lighting of the National Menorah on the Ellipse. Dates vary from year depending on when the eight-day festival of Chanukah begins.

National Christmas Tree Lighting and Pageant of Peace
www.whitehouse.gov

Every holiday season an online lottery is held for the chance to see the President of The United States light the National Christmas Tree on the Ellipse. The Tree Lighting event is marked with concerts, storytelling, and the Pageant of Peace. To enter the lottery, visit the White House's website in early November for details. Even if you are not a lucky winner, you can still visit the tree and enjoy the nightly concerts offered throughout the season.

Scottish Christmas Walk Weekend & Parade
www.scottishchristmaswalk.com

Celebrate the holiday season and Alexandria's Scottish heritage with a Christmas Marketplace at George Washington Masonic Memorial, a Holiday Designer Tour of Homes, and the famous Scottish Walk Parade with 100 Scottish clans dressed in tartans and playing bagpipes, dog clubs and antique cars.

U.S. Botanical Gardens Season's Greenings
www.usbg.gov/exhibits

The garden's stunning annual holiday display with festive plants, an ornate model train display, and recreations of the National Mall and monuments is magically created using plant-based materials.

It is an awe-inspiring walk through a fantasyland not to be missed! Lines can get long to enter this popular display, so try to arrive early.

ZooLights
www.nationalzoo.si.edu

Every December the National Zoo is transformed into a magical, winter wonderland with more than 500,000 environmentally friendly LED lights. Get a free photo with "Panda Claws" and be sure not to miss the large "Wildlife Train Park" model train display in the visitors' center. Many animal exhibits are open throughout the program. The event is free but add-ons like parking, food, tubing, the carousel and train ride require extra fees.

Chapter 25

Family Fun Across the Potomac

Chapter 25: Family Fun Across the Potomac

1. Get Wild With Wildlife

Audubon Naturalist Society's Woodend
8940 Jones Mill Road
Chevy Chase, MD
301-652-9188
www.audubonnaturalist.org

Take a bird walk, walk through a wildflower meadow, follow meandering trails, and explore aquatic pond-life at the historic 40-acre Woodend sanctuary. The Woodend Mansion is an admired example of the Georgian Revival and is one of the last remaining grand old estates in Chevy Chase. Nature programs are held for children and families throughout the year. Free admission.

Smithsonian National Zoological Park
3001 Connecticut Avenue
202-633-4462
www.nationalzoo.si.edu

The Smithsonian National Zoological Park is a beautiful 163-acre urban park offering family fun and excitement, kid-friendly educational programs, and a great introduction for your little ones to over 2,000 animals from around the world. Popular recent additions to the Zoo include a Kid's Farm, Carousel, and Zoo Choo-Choo. Admission is free; parking is $16 for the first 3 hours. On busy weekends, parking fills up quickly so a better option is to take the Metro or utilize the new parking reservation system by calling Guest Services to reserve a spot. Although food vendors are located throughout the Zoo if the kids are willing, treat yourself to lunch at one of the nearby trendy restaurants on Connecticut Avenue.

The National Aquarium
1401 Constitution Avenue, NW
Washington, DC 20230
202-482-2825
www.nationalaquarium.org

Although the National Aquarium is much smaller than its Baltimore counterpart, young children will enjoy tanks of more than 250 species of alligators, piranhas, and sharks. Strollers are allowed, but space is tight. Located close to the National Mall and in the Department of Commerce building since 1932, the space received a complete renovation in 2008. Tots and Tales program for children held every 1st and 3rd Friday of the month from 10-11 a.m.

Rock Creek Park
5200 Glover Road, NW
Washington, DC 20015
www.nps.gov/rocr

In addition to extensive trails, Rock Creek Park has a fun Nature Center, a kids' Discovery Room, hands on activities that teach about the park's ecosystem, and a 75-seat planetarium. On the way out, kids can pick-up a discovery pack equipped with binoculars, a magnifying lens and bird identification chart to use on a trail hike. At the Rock Creek Park Stables, kids can also take a pony ride (best for preschoolers) or an hour-long trail ride through the woods (best for elementary school aged children and up). Call the Stables in advance for reservations and availability.

2. Visit the Smithsonian Museums

There are 16 Smithsonian Museums in the DC Metro area filled with educational pursuits that will entertain the whole family. The Smithsonian museums offer free admission and are easily accessible via Metro. Plus, the majority of museums are clustered together on the National Mall to allow you to easily make a full day of your Smithsonian journey. For a welcome break, visit one of the museum cafes or stroll over to the Carousel on the Mall. An IMAX movie at the Natural History or Air & Space Museum or a children's show at Discovery Theatre also make for a nice scheduled break. Here is a list of our favorite Smithsonian picks for the little ones:

Hirshorn Museum & Sculpture Garden
Independence Avenue at 7th Street, SW
Washington, DC 20560
www.hirshhorn.si.edu

This museum of modern and contemporary art is a great place to introduce children to art. The wide open spaces vivid visual images and three-dimensional sculptural works delight even the youngest toddlers. In the summer the outdoor sculpture garden hosts a series of free concerts that are perfect for an evening picnic.

National Air & Space Museum
Independence Avenue at 7th Street, SW
Washington, DC 20560
202-357-2700
www.nasm.si.edu

This can be an incredible visit for a youngster that is interested in flight. The museum vividly outlines the history of air and space travel starting with Orville and Wilber Wright and advancing to NASA''s history. For even more fun sit in a real cockpit, take a simulator ride, and enjoy and IMAX movie.

National Museum of Natural History
10th Street & Constitution Avenue
Washington, DC 20560
202-633-1000
www.mnh.si.edu

The National Museum of Natural History (NMNH) is dedicated to inspiring curiosity discovery and learning about the natural world. First stops are usually Dinosaur Hall and Sea Life Hall, but kids will also be fascinated by the rare gem displays. For interactive fun head to the Insect Zoo and Discovery Room where kids can feel the skin of a crocodile, examine animal teeth, and try on costumes.

National Museum of the American Indian
Fourth Street & Independence Avenue, SW
Washington, DC 20560
202-633-1000
www.nmai.si.edu

The National Museum of the American Indian hosts an impressive collection of Native American artifacts, costumes, multi-media displays, and hands on exhibits for children. The cafeteria boasts amazing Native American cuisines from different tribes and attracts tourists and locals alike.

National Postal Museum
2 Massachusetts Avenue
Washington DC 20002
202-357-2700
http://www.postalmuseum.si.edu

The galleries of the National Postal Museum explore America's postal history from colonial times to the present. Visitors learn how mail has been transported emphasize the importance of letters and spotlight the creation and wondrous diversity of postage stamps.

3. Enjoy a Kid-Friendly Show

Atlas Performing Arts Center
1333 H Street, NE
Washington, DC 20002
202-399-7993
www.atlasarts.org

The Atlas hosts a variety of programs for children throughout the year including the Capital City Symphony's popular Annual Family Concert, performances by the Theatre for the Very Young, and performances by the American Youth Chorus.

Discovery Theatre
1100 Jefferson Drive, SW
Washington, DC 20024
202-633-8700
www.discoverytheater.org

The Smithsonian's Theatre for Young Children offers a variety of family programming ranging from science demonstrations to kiddie rock to puppet shows. Weekday shows are usually held at 10:15 a.m. and 11:30 a.m. Check the schedule for special weekend performances and programs.

Imagination Stage
4908 Auburn Avenue
Bethesda, MD 20814
301-961-6060
www.imaginationstage.org

Imagination Stage is the largest theatre arts organization for young people in the Mid-Atlantic region. They offer a year-round season of terrific shows, after-school programs, and summer camps.

Kennedy Center Millennium Stage
2700 F Street NW
Washington, DC 20566
202-467-4600
www.kennedy-center.org/programs/millennium/

The Kennedy Center's Millennium Stage offers free shows in a variety of different performance arts daily at 6 p.m. Some performances require advance (free) tickets.

Saturday Morning at the National Theatre
1321 Pennsylvania Avenue, NW
Washington, DC 20004
www.nationaltheatre.org

On a seasonal basis, the National Theatre opens up its doors for free family shows Saturday mornings at 9:30 and 11:00 a.m. Free tickets are distributed ½ hour prior to show time.

4. Take an Outing to National Harbor

Just south of Alexandria on the Potomac, the giant new complex of National Harbor boasts more than 70 shops and restaurants, six hotels, outdoor concert venue, a marina and the new National Children's Museum. Enjoy waterfront dining, take a pedal boat, kayak, or sightseeing cruise out on the river, and treat the kids to a visit to the National Children's Museum. Restless kids will also enjoy a walk along the waterfront, a stop at Ben & Jerry's for ice cream, and exploring the gargantuan statue "The Awakening." Special events, fireworks, concerts, movies, and athletic events are scheduled throughout the year.

5. Visit Historic Glen Echo Amusement Park

Glen Echo Park
7300 MacArthur Blvd.
Glen Echo, MD 20812
301-634-2222
www.glenechopark.org

A national park dedicated to preserving arts and culture, this former amusement park hosts a variety of family activities from family dancing and artist workshops to world-class children's shows by Adventure Theatre and the Puppet Co.. The Dentzel Carousel, installed in 1921, is a beautiful centerpiece and attraction for the young and old. At the Living Classroom, children can learn about nature, meet with different animals, and participate in hands on activities. In between activities families can take a walk in the woods along the C&O canal, picnic in the covered picnic area, or play at the playground. Restrooms and vending machines are available. Special events are scheduled throughout the year.

6. Tour the Monuments

The Jefferson Memorial
701 West Basin Drive, SW
Washington DC 20242
202-426-6841
www.nps.gov/thje

Sitting at the southern end of the National Mall, the Thomas Jefferson Memorial and Tidal Basin are most visited during the annual Cherry Blossom Festival, but are wonderful destinations year-round. See the grandeur of the Thomas Jefferson statue, stroll amid the cherry trees along the Tidal Basin, rent a paddleboat or simply enjoy the view from the steps of the Jefferson Memorial. Restrooms, a gift shop and a small museum are located within the base of the memorial. Bring a picnic or purchase food and ice cream from local vendors along the Tidal Basin.

The Lincoln Memorial
2 Memorial Circle NW
Washington, DC 20037
202-426-6841
www.nps.gov/linc

It could be that kids relate to the fatherly statue of the seated Lincoln or the legendary stories of young Abe growing up in a log cabin, but whatever the reason, the Lincoln Memorial makes a big impact on kids. Climbing the steps and reading the 16th President's words is an inspiring experience for all.

The Washington Memorial
15th Street, NW
Washington, DC 20007
202-426-6841
www.nps.gov/wamo

The Washington Monument offers an amazing view from the top. Tickets are required, but are free. Tickets are distributed daily at 8:30 AM. However, during popular weekends and holidays, folks line up as early as 7:30 AM. Therefore, your best bet is to go during weekdays or off-peak hours. [NOTE: The Washington Monument may still be closed for repairs from an earthquake in 2011. At time of publication, reopening date was still unlisted.]

Martin Luther King Jr. National Memorial
www.nps.gov/mlkm

The impressive new Martin Luther King Jr. National Memorial stands on a four-acre plot along the Tidal Basin and creates a visual "line of leadership" from the Lincoln Memorial to the Jefferson Memorial. The statute of Dr. King emerging from the large granite stone embodies his resolve to achieve equality for all. Interpretive programs are offered on the site every hour from 10:00 a.m. until 11:00 p.m.

7. Take a Boat Ride

Boathouse at Fletcher's Cove
4940 Canal Road, NW
Washington, DC 20007
202-244-0461
http://www.fletcherscove.com/

Capitol River Cruises
Washington Harbour
Washington, DC 20007
800-405-5511
www.capitolrivercruises.com

C&O Canal National Historical Park Boat Rides
www.nps.gov/choh/planyourvisit/publicboatrides.htm

D.C. Ducks
Union Station
Washington, DC 20018
855-323-8257
www.dcducks.com

Odyssey Cruises
600 Water Street, SW
Washington, DC 20024
866-306-2469
www.odysseycruises.com

Spirit of Washington Cruise
600 Water Street, SW
Washington, DC 20024
866-302-2469
www.spiritofwashington.com

Thompson Boat Center
2900 Virginia Avenue, NW
Washington, DC 20037
202-333-9543
www.thompsonboatcenter.com

Tidal Basin Paddle Boats
1501 Maine Avenue, SW
Washington, DC 20024
www.tidalbasinpaddleboats.com

8. Explore a Garden

Brookside Gardens
1800 Glenallan Avenue
Wheaton, MD 20902
301-962-1400
www.montgomeryparks.org/brookside

Brookside Gardens is an award-winning 50-acre public display garden situated within Montgomery County's Wheaton Regional Park. Included in the gardens are several distinct areas: Aquatic Garden, Azalea Garden, Butterfly Garden, Children's Garden, Rose Garden, Japanese Style Garden, Trial Garden, Rain Garden and the Woodland Walk. The gardens make a wonderful setting for a stroll, picnic, and family photo. Brookside Gardens also feature two conservatories for year-round enjoyment. The nearby nature center has special exhibits for children. In the warmer months, Brookside hosts the Wings of Fancy Live Butterfly Exhibit (the best encounter with butterflies you will find in the area) and in the winter the Gardens are lit with thousands of outdoor lights during the enchanting Garden of Lights display.

Dumbarton Oaks
1703 32nd Street, NW
Washington, DC 20007
202-339-6410
www.doaks.org

The beautiful 10-acre gardens are a lovely retreat in the heart of Georgetown and perfect place to take a stroll. Walking on the grass is discouraged, so you may want to take children elsewhere for active play. Also note, no picnicking or pets allowed. The museum houses a fascinating collection of pre-Columbian and Byzantine art. Street parking only.

Hillwood Estate Museum and Gardens
4155 Linnean Avenue, NW
Washington, DC 20008
202-686-8500
www.hillwoodmuseum.org

Heiress to the Post cereal fortune, Marjorie Merriweather Post created an oasis of formal gardens and fine art in one of the loveliest parts of DC. Now open to the public, her 25-acre estate features a world-class garden architecture, sculpture, a Japanese garden with waterfall and bridge, a rose garden, fishponds, more than 3,500 varieties of plants and trees, and a greenhouse containing more than 5,000 orchids. Children especially enjoy following winding paths through the gardens and balancing on stepping-stones across the Japanese garden. The museum houses one of the country's premier art collections of French art and furnishings, Russian imperial art, and Faberge eggs. Lunch is available at the Hillwood Cafe. Hillwood is especially pretty in the spring and makes a wonderful mother's day destination. Note: strollers must be checked at the entrance. The venue will loan out baby carriers.

Tudor Place
1644 31st Street, NW
Washington, DC 20007
www.tudorplace.org

Built in 1816 by Martha Washington's granddaughter, the historic neoclassical estate houses a collection of decorative arts and is surrounded by five-acres of formal gardens featuring a Bowling Green, Tennis Lawn, Flower Knot, Boxwood Ellipse, Japanese Tea House and Tulip Poplar. Also highly recommended: Tudor Place's seasonal Georgetown Civil War House & Walking Tours, popular Summer Camps and Workshops for children, Tuesday Teas, and Tastings.

United States National Arboretum
3501 New York Avenue, NE
Washington, DC 20002
202-245-2726
www.usna.usda.gov

A 35-minute tram tour highlights the 446-acres of the Arboretum's gardens, collections, and natural areas. Although visitors are welcome to hike the grounds, the closest and easiest areas to walk through are the Aquatic Garden and Koi Pond, the Friendship Garden, the National Herb Garden, and the National Bonsai & Penjing Museum. A gift shop and snacks are available for visitors. Picnicking allowed only in designated areas.

United States Botanic Garden
100 Maryland Avenue Southwest
Washington, DC 20024
202-225-8333
www.usbg.gov

The United States Botanic Garden (USBG) is located on the U.S. Capitol Grounds campus near Garfield Circle. The building itself, which includes a large Lord & Burnham greenhouse, is divided into separate rooms, each one simulating a different habitat. The USBG offers endless activities for kids and adults. Children will learn valuable lessons about plants, gardening and many interesting facts about the world of botany. The USBG can make a great starting or ending point if you are planning for a day on the National Mall. It can also be welcome retreat on a cold or rainy day!

9. Show Your Team Spirit

DC United (Soccer)
RFK Stadium
2400 East Capitol Street, SE
Washington, DC 20003
202-587-5000
www.dcunited.com

Washington Capitals (Hockey)
Verizon Center
601 F Street, NW
Washington, DC 20004
202-628-3200
http://capitals.nhl.com/

Washington Kastles (Tennis)
800 Water Street, SW
Washington, DC 20024
202-4-TENNIS
www.washingtonkastles.com

Washington Mystics (Women's Basketball)
Verizon Center
601 F Street, NW
Washington, DC 20004
202-628-3200
www.wnba.com/mystics

Washington Nationals (Baseball)
Nationals Park
1500 South Capitol Street, SE
Washington, DC 20003
202-675-6287
http://washington.nationals.mlb.com/index.jsp?c_id=was

Washington Redskins (Football)
FedEx Field
1600 Fedex Way
Landover, MD 20785
301-276-6000
www.redskins.com

Washington Spirit (Women's Soccer)
18031 Central Park Circle
Boyds, MD 20841
240-813-2695
www.washingtonspirit.com

Washington Wizards (Basketball)
Verizon Center
601 F Street, NW
Washington, DC 20004
202-628-3200
www.nba.com

10. Enjoy Tween and Teen-Friendly Fun

Adventure Park at Sandy Spring Friends School
16701 Norwood Road
Sandy Spring MD 20860
240.389.4386
www.sandyspringadventurepark.org

North America's largest aerial adventure park has 180 Challenges, 25 zip lines, 12 courses, and six difficulty levels. Open 7 days a week during the summer. A child as young as five can climb the easiest course, but as the difficulty of the courses increases, so does the thrill factor. An absolutely exhilarating experience for anyone who dares to lock-in!

International Spy Museum
800 F Street, NW
Washington, DC 20004
202-EYE-SPYU
www.spymuseum.org

Get your would-be spies ready for a great adventure! The Spy Museum if filled with over 200 spy gadgets, weapons, bugs, cameras, vehicles, and technologies. Guests can peek at over 50 years of spy technologies created by agencies such as the CIA and the KGB.

Discover little known facts about notorious spies such as Moses, Harriet Tubman, Elizabeth I to George Washington, Cardinal Richelieu, Joseph Stalin and more. The venue offers summer day camps and special events for kids throughout the year.

Madame Tussaud's Wax Museum
1001 F Street
Washington, DC 20004
www.madametussauds.com/washington

Have you ever wanted to kiss Brad Pitt? Give Muhammed Ali a big ole hug? Or simply see if you were taller than George Washington? Madame Tussauds Washington DC is the place to do it all. Visitors can get close to major historical figures and celebrities in a way unlike any other.

Maloof Skatepark at RFK Stadium
2400 E. Capitol Street, SE
Washington, DC 20003

This outdoor 15,000-square-foot skate park is the first major skate park in Washington DC and is inspired by Freedom Plaza and the architecture along Pennsylvania Avenue. The primary skate park entrance is from Lot 3. When Lot 3 is closed, the skate park entrance is on East Capitol Street. Free parking in Lot 3 and 5.

National Geographic Explorers Hall
17th & M Streets NW
Washington DC 20036
www.nationalgeographic.com/nglive

This high tech exhibit hall on the ground floor of National Geographic's headquarters features interactive exhibits, world-class photography, and displays exploring nature and humanity across the globe. Check the website for featured films lectures concerts and family events.

National Museum of Crime & Punishment
575 7th Street, NW
Washington, DC
www.crimemuseum.org

Described by Good Morning America as a "must see for CSI fans" this museum includes a crime lab and the filming studios for America's Most Wanted. Expect to find a simulated shooting range, high-speed police-chase, and hundreds of interactive exhibits and artifacts pertaining to America's favorite subject. This is one museum that even your tween will enjoy...but wait to bring your littlest ones. The Museum also does birthday parties, workshops, and camps.

National Museum of Health and Medicine
2500 Linden Lane
Silver Spring, MD 20910
http://www.medicalmuseum.mil/

This museum houses a collection of fascinating (and sometimes gory) specimens collected since the Civil War. Although many of the more controversial jars have been put in storage, be judicious in deciding whether your children are ready to see preserved body parts and fascinating exhibits depicting malformations, traumatic wartime injuries, and diseases.

Newseum
555 Pennsylvania Avenue, NW
Washington, DC 20001
888-639-7386
www.newseum.org

The Newseum is Washington's largest interactive museum with 14 major galleries and 15 theaters that immerse you in the world's greatest news stories. Highlights include 8 concrete sections of the Berlin Wall, the 9/11 Gallery, the Watergate Door, Pulitzer Prize-winning Photographs, the Unabomber's Cabin, interactive newsrooms, and a 4-D Time Travel Adventure that recreates the most dramatic events in journalism history. Finally don't miss the Greenspun Family Terrace, which offers one of the best panoramic views of the Capitol and DC monuments.

United States Holocaust Memorial Museum
100 Raoul Wallenberg Place, SW
Washington DC
202-488-0400
http://www.ushmm.org

The permanent exhibit at the Holocaust Memorial Museum houses more than 900 artifacts, 70 video monitors, and four theaters showing film footage and eyewitness testimonies of Nazi concentration camp survivors. Images of death and destruction are graphic and, therefore, this museum is not recommended for children under 11 years old.

Chapter 26

Kid Trips Top Picks

Chapter 26: Kid Trips Top Picks

Best Party Locations

American Girl Doll Store
80901 Tysons Corner Center
McLean, VA 22102
www.americangirl.com

You have officially found heaven for most girls between the ages of 3 and 13. Even parents who have begrudgingly given into the American Girl phenomenon will be impressed. The shop is a two-story wonderland of American Girl dolls, clothes, books, DVDs and other accessories. Lucky party-goers can either bring their own doll or borrow one for the duration of the celebration. Party packages include a host of options including a trip to the Doll Hair Salon, a Bistro Birthday Celebration, or a Deluxe Birthday Celebration that includes a private table in the bistro, a craft activity and a take home goodie bag. Birthday parties are for ages 3 and up.

APEX Gymnastics
741 Miller Drive, SE
Leesburg, VA 20175-8994
703-777-5344
http://apexgymn.com

With the recent success of USA Gymnastics, the sport has taken off locally. While you may not want to commit to years of training, a birthday party might be just perfect for your little tumbler. APEX offers high-energy 90-minute parties that include an instructor, games, trampoline time, and an obstacle course. Each child receives a special ribbon and the birthday boy or girl will receive a trophy. They even have invitations available. There are a number of custom packages available at different price points. The "Platinum Party" includes a cake, pizza, drinks and place settings and gym time. Moon bounces can be added for a nominal fee. Parties are geared for children ages 4-12.

Apollo Gymnastics
12700 Apollo Drive
Woodbridge, VA 22192
703-580-9144
http://apollogymnasticsva.com

Party packages include a skilled instructor, games, trampoline time, an obstacle course and a party room. Parties are geared for children ages 4-12. Parents must bring party supplies and food.

Cookology
Dulles Town Center
21100 Dulles Town Circle
Dulles, VA 20166
www.cookologyonline.com

Cookology parties offer kids a delicious way to celebrate their birthday. As part of the party guests don a chef's hat and apron and prepare their own food and desserts with help from the chefs. The birthday girl or boy can choose a custom menu from kid-friendly favorites like mac and cheese or homemade pizzas. Balloons and themed goody bags with fun chef tools are available for an extra cost. Parties are available for kids ages 4-15.

Curiosity Zone
43135 Broadlands Center Plaza, Suite 123
Ashburn, VA 20148
703-723-9949
http://www.curiosityzone.com/

Science concoctions, UFO balls, smoke rings, and more await you at Curiosity Zone. Located in the heart of Ashburn, Curiosity Zone offers parents a 90-minute party filled with experiments, activities and a pint sized science lab with test tubes, beakers and more! Parents bring the food, cake and supplies. Kids create their own fun drinks. C-Zone supplies utensils, plates, balloons and festive science-themed goodie bags. An array of fun party themes are offered for children ages 2 - 10.

Frying Pan Park's Kidwell Farm
2709 West Ox Road
Herndon, VA 20171
703-437-9101
http://www.fairfaxcounty.gov/

Whether the season calls for a "Barnyard Bash" or a climate controlled party room, Frying Pan Farm Park is the perfect place to have a party for your little animal lover. Parties are tiered for different budgets and can include a 30 minute guided program and/or a private wagon ride for guests. Goody bags containing Frying Pan Farm park trinkets and old-fashioned candy can be purchased at extra cost. For those looking to save money, consider renting the classroom in the visitors' center or a picnic pavilion and then visit the farm (which is free) with your party guests.

Harmony Road Music & Art
6101 Redwood Square Centre #119
Centreville, VA 20121
http://www.harmonyroadva.com

Harmony is perfect for your little Renaissance boy or girl who wants to mix music and art with a birthday celebration. Children are treated to a music or art party themed celebration that is lead by one of the Harmony Road instructors. Food, utensils, drinks and a birthday cake are all provided.

Heritage Farm Museum
21668 Heritage Farm Lane
Sterling, VA 20164
571-258-3800
www.heritagefarmmuseum.org/birthday.htm

A fantastic and affordable place for toddler and preschool birthday parties, the Heritage Farm offers a basic package of a two-hour party for up to ten children and five adults. The party includes museum admission, use of the cute and clean party cabin for three hours, and goody bags for the children. The birthday child will receive a special birthday toy. Additional add-ons such as a guided program, craft, and story time are extra.

ideaventions™ - A Discovery Lab for Kids
2952-H Chain Bridge Road
Oakton, VA 22124
703-255-7202
www.ideaventions.com

Ideaventions offers an interactive party experience for children ages 3-13. Unique party themes include: Ancient Egypt, Construction, Cars, Dinosaurs, Fairy Magic, Pirates, Robotics, Space, Secret Agents, Spa, Undersea, Veterinarian and Whodunity. This is a unique alternative for a birthday gathering. While party packages offer drinks, parents must bring the food. With educational and imaginative activities, this is a party experience that is sure to please both kids and parents.

Jumping Jacks Sports
44710 Cape Court
Ashburn, VA 20147
703-858-9901
www.jumpingjacksports.com/

Jumping Jack Sports offers a number of party packages with access to the Main Gym and Party Room. Parties have a sports theme that can include playtime on huge inflatables, plasma cars, rock walls and plenty of organized sports options. Your group is lead by "coaches" that help with party set-up, leading events and clean-up. Paper products, drinks, and a keepsake wristband are all provided. You will need to provide the food and cake. This spot is best for ages 3 to tween.

Lifetime Fitness
Fairfax, Sterling and Centreville
www.lifetimefitness.com

Lifetime offers rock climbing, an indoor playspace with moon bounces or an outdoor pool party package. The possibilities are endless in this massive gym. Non-members pay a slightly higher rate for birthday parties. Parties are best for children ages 3 - 12.

Little Gym (The)
Ashburn, Alexandria Huntley Meadows, Alexandria Van Dorn, Fairfax, Falls Church, Gainesville
www.thelittlegym.com

The LittleGym is perfect for younger children. Run, jump, play and celebrate with a lively instructor, just the right-sized gymnastic equipment, and lots of games and activities. Partygoers take over the facility and celebrate with games, music and fun activities. The Little Gym handles everything from set-up to clean-up.

My Gym
Alexandria, Burke and Chantilly
www.mygym.com

My Gym offers a fun, open area where kids can run, jump and play all under the watchful eye of a trained instructor. Studios have climbing structures, ball pits, gymnastics equipment, and more. There are three different party packages to choose from for your celebration. Set-up, decorations and clean-up are all provided. You will need to bring the food, drinks and party products.

nZone
14550 Lee Road
Chantilly, VA 20151
703-226-0118
www.thenzone.com

nZone is a great birthday venue option for sports-minded children. It offers a variety of party packages that range from soccer to lacrosse. They even offer dodgeball for adults. Parents can choose between a wood or turf court with a referee, a skills trainer or a facilitator. Packages include a semi-private room, cake, pizza, utensils, paper products and a goody bag for each guest. Add-ons such as moon bounces are available.

Pump It Up
Leesburg & Manassas
www.pumpitupparty.com

This is a fun venue that is always a crowd pleaser. The helpful and friendly staff helps children navigate the many slides, bounce houses and obstacle courses. Kids are led through two rooms of fun and then into a private room for cake and, if requested, food. Parties can book quickly and be aware that you may be sharing slide time with other groups of partygoers.

Tiny Dancers
Alexandria, Fairfax and Gainesville
www.tinydancers.com

If your little one is yearning for a fairy tale birthday party, then Tiny Dancers is your answer. Partygoers will enjoy special costumes, craft activity, and story time complete with a dance lesson. Parents can select from over fifty different ballet stories for the dance portion of the party. Packages include a 90-minute party, cake, drinks, goodie bags and party supplies. All you need is the tiara! Tiny Dancers is best suited for ages 2 - 12.

Ultrazone Laser Tag & Amusement Center
3447 Carlin Springs Road
Falls Church, VA 22041
www.ultralasertag.com

Ultrazone Laser Tag & Amusement Center is perfect for kids and tweens who have aged out of the preschool party circuit. Participants compete for points in a dark labyrinth filled with a light, smoky fog. Games last 30 minutes and are filled with action and excitement. Private rooms, pizza, cake, utensils and invitations are included in birthday party packages. Come armed with money for tokens: in between laser tournaments kids will want to play video games in the arcade.

Best Consignment Shops

529 Kids Consign
122 A. South Royal Street
Alexandria, VA 22314
www.529kidsconsign.com

Bellies & Babies
1913 Mt. Vernon Avenue
Alexandria, VA 22301
703-518-8908
www.belliesbabies.com

Chic Envy Consignment
11895 Grand Commons Avenue
Fairfax, VA 22030
703-268-5228
www.chicenvy.com

Chic Envy Consignment
7937 Stonewall Shops Square
Gainesville, VA 20155
703-743-9577
www.chicenvy.com

Frilly Frocks
The Village at Leesburg
1603 Village Market Boulevard SE
Leesburg, VA 20175
703-858-4940
www.frillyfrocks.com

Kid to Kid Centreville
6039 Centreville Crest Lane
Centreville, VA 20121703-222-4595
www.kidtokid.com/centreville

Little Lords and Ladies
14088 Sullyfield Circle
Chantilly, VA 20151
703-488-9948
www.littlelordsandladies.com

Paddington Station
448 Maple Ave East
Vienna, VA 22180
703-938-0378

Small Change Consignments
1629 Washington Plaza
Reston, Virginia 20190
703-437-7730
www.smallchangeconsignments.com

Treasured Child
9411-C Old Burke Lake Road
Burke, VA 22015
703-978-4778

Unique
2956 Gallows Road
Falls Church, VA 22042
703-992-6569
www.imunique.com/

Best Kids' Haircuts

Andy's Barber Shop
431 Maple Ave West, Suite D
Vienna, VA 22180
703-255-7131
www.andysbarbershop.blogspot.com

Tucked away in an unassuming strip mall in Vienna, Andy's Barber Shop is a secret that all the locals know about but seldom seem to share. All week long the shop has a steady stream of customers both young and old. The owner Andy and his staff are very welcoming and there is a small area with kids' toys as well as an aquarium. While you won't find a TV at every chair they do move quickly and end with a lollipop for the little ones. I have taken my daughter in for a quick $8.00 bang trim. We were happy with the trim, but the place tends to be more geared toward the boys.

Cartoon Cuts
Dulles Town Center, Fair Oaks Mall and Smoketown Station
www.cartooncuts.com

With three area locations, Cartoon Cuts is a kid-favorite. The staff is very experienced with children and kids get so absorbed in watching their own personal TV screen that they forget they are getting a haircut.

Insider Tip: Don't be afraid to ask the hairdresser to change the show. They have a large stock of DVDs with most major characters represented.

Eclips Kids
42395 Ryan Road
Ashburn, VA
703-327-9408
www.eclipshair.com

This salon offers high quality hair care products for children. They also offer hair styling for special occasions and participate in the Locks of Love program.

Best Ice Cream and Frozen Yogurt Shops

BR Frozen Custard and Sweets
4125 Merchant Plaza
Woodbridge, VA 22192
www.brfudge.com

Coldstone Creamery
Multiple Locations in Northern Virginia
www.coldstonecreamery.com

The Dairy Godmother
2310 Mount Vernon Avenue
Alexandria, VA 22301
www.thedairygodmother.com

Frozen Dairy Bar
6649 Arlington Boulevard
Falls Church, VA 22042
www.fdbpizza.com

Josie's Frozen Yogurt
10625 Braddock Road
Fairfax, VA 22032
571-490-7780
www.josiesyogurt.com

Mike's Deli at Lazy Sundae
110 N. West Street
Falls Church, VA 22046
www.mikesdeliatlazysundae.com

Milwaukee Custard
Ashburn, Chantilly, Herndon, Leesburg and Woodbridge
www.milwaukeefrozencustard.com

Nielsens Frozen Custard
114 Church Street
Vienna, VA 22180
www.thecustardstore.com

Pinkberry Frozen Yogurt
Arlington, Clarendon Center, Fairfax, Leesburg and McLean
www.pinkberry.com

Peterson's Ice Cream Depot
7150 Main Street
Clifton, VA 20124
703-830-7898
www.petersonsdepot.com

Pop's Old Fashioned Ice Cream
109 King Street
Alexandria, VA 22314
www.fishmarketva.com/index.php?/pops

Rita's Water Ice
Alexandria, Chantilly, Fairfax, Fredericksburg & Woodbridge
www.ritasice.com

Sweet Berry
9432 Main Street
Fairfax,VA 22031
www.sweetberryusa.com

Scoop Grill & Homemade Ice Cream
110 King Street
Alexandria, VA 22314

Woody's Ice Cream
10435 North Street
Fairfax, VA 22030
www.woodysicecream.com

Yolly Molly Café
12164 Fairfax Town Center
Fairfax, VA 22033
www.yollymolly.com

Yogen Fruz
Tysons Corner Center
1961 Chain Bridge Road
McLean, VA 22102

Yogen Fruz
Potomac Mills
2700 Potomac Mills Circle
Woodbridge, VA 22192
www.yogenfruz.com

Best Baby Goods & Toy Stores

Each of these stores is locally owned and stocked with impressive, unique merchandise.

Apple Seed Maternity and Baby
115 S. Columbus Street
Alexandria, VA 22314
703-535-5446
www.appleseedboutique.com

Baby Blossom
9512 Main Street
Fairfax VA 22031
703-865-4688
www.babyblossom.homestead.com

Baby Blossom
1631 Washington Plaza
Reston, Virginia 20190
571-313-1717
www.babyblossom.homestead.com

Barstons Child's Play Toy Store
4510 Lee Highway
Arlington, VA 22207
703-522-1022

Barstons Child's Play Toy Store
Langley Shopping Center
1382 Chainbridge Rd
Mclean, VA 22101
703-448-3444
www.barstonschildsplay.com

Dawn Price Baby
2905 District Ave, Suite 120
Fairfax, VA 22031
703-992-6533
www.dawnpricebaby.com

Dawn Price Baby
11985 Market Street
Reston, VA 20190
703-787-3040
www.dawnpricebaby.com

Doodlehopper 4 Kids Toy Store
7521 Huntsman Blvd
Springfield, VA 22153
703-912-7200
www.doodlehopper.com

Doodlehopper 4 Kids Toy Store
228 West Broad Street
Falls Church, VA 22046
703-241-2262
www.doodlehopper.com

Great Beginnings
13920 Lee Jackson Memorial Highway
Chantilly, VA 20151
571-512-4280
www.greatbeginningsonline.com

Go Bananas Toy Store
42395 Ryan Road
Ashburn, VA 20148
703 327-1900
www.gobananastoys.com

Go Bananas Toy Store
19352 Promenade Drive
Leesburg VA 20176
571-333-4514
www.gobananastoys.com

Kinder Haus Toys
1220 N. Fillmore Street
Arlington, VA 22201
703-527-5929
www.kinderhaus.com

One, Two Kangaroo Toys
4022 Campbell Avenue
Arlington, VA 22206
703-845-9099
www.villageatshirlington.com/shopping/specialty/one-two-kangaroo-toys/

Purple Goose (The)
2005 Mt. Vernon Avenue
Alexandria, VA 22301
703-683-2918
www.thepurplegoose.com

The Tabby Cat
Hunter Mill Plaza
2946-F Chain Bridge Road
Oakton, VA 22124
703-255-0812
www.tabbycatkids.com

Toy Corner
2930 Chain Bridge Road
Oakton, VA 22124
703-537-5808

Why Not?
200 King Street
Alexandria, VA 22314
703-548-4420
www.alexandriacitywebsite.com/WhyNot.htm

Top Ten Kid-Friendly Restaurants

Blue Ridge Grill
Leesburg and Brambleton
www.brgrill.com

The Blue Ridge Grill serves up healthy portions of casual, fresh food. Kids' menu options also include fried shrimp, grilled salmon, ribs, and filet mignon. The adult menu has plenty of fun choices, and the restaurants are also open for weekend brunch.

Celebrity Delly
7263-A Arlington Boulevard
Falls Church, VA 22042
703-573-9002
www.celebritydeliva.com

"The Celebrity Delly" (not "deli") is right on par with those found in New York and features great breakfasts, amazing sandwiches, and catering options. Definitely the best place around to get a hot pastrami or matzo ball soup. This is a perfect family-friendly stop if you are heading into Washington D.C. via Route 50.

Dixie Bones
13440 Occoquan Road
Woodbridge, VA 22191
703-492-2205
www.dixiebones.com

Continuously acclaimed as one of the best BBQ places in the area, Dixie Bones has an extensive menu. Kids plates are served with an apple and fries, but families can also order family-style entrees and sides. Dixie Bones is also known for their large Sunday brunch.

Eat Bar
2751 Washington Boulevard
Arlington, VA 22201
703-778-5150
www.eat-bar.com

This American Gastropub serves up unique dishes such as bacon popcorn balls, fried green tomatoes, lamb burgers, and chicken with waffles. Although there is no designated children's menu, kids can order small plates and sliders. Eat Bar is known for its "Cartoon Brunch" every Sunday from 10 a.m. - 2:30 p.m. that shows classic cartoons on the big screen. Located walking distance from the Clarendon Metro.

Fish Market (The)
105 King Street
Alexandria, VA 22314
703-836-5676
www.fishmarketva.com

A great location just steps away from the waterfront in Old Town Alexandria, The Fish Market consistently serves up fresh seafood in a casual atmosphere. The kids' menu includes fried shrimp, fish & chips, as well as "land lubber" fare. Don't forget to stop in Pop's Old Fashioned Ice Cream next door, also owned by The Fish Market family.

Generous George's
2321-C Dulles Station Boulevard
Herndon, VA 20171
703-793-3338
www.generousgeorges.com

Families can enjoy casual pizza and pasta dishes in a fun decorated dining room. The kid's menu has a "make your own pizza" option that comes with a chef's hat to take home. Kids love it!

Great American Restaurants
Multiple Locations in Northern Virginia
www.greatamericanrestaurants.com

This fantastic local franchise includes twelve restaurants in the NoVA area, each with a unique theme: Ozzie's is Italian, Coastal Flats features Southern-style seafood, Sweetwater is a fun cowboy-themed American brewery, etc. Dishes are consistently high quality, and kids' menus have good options such as salmon stacks, quesadillas, and grouper fingers (selection varies by location). With their lively atmospheres and friendly staff, any of the locations are a good bet for families.

Greene Turtle (The)
www.thegreeneturtle.com

A DC/MD/VA franchise with locations in Arlington, Fairfax, Fredericksburg, Leesburg, and Sterling, The Greene Turtle is a family favorite that serves casual fare such as burgers, wings, and sandwiches as well as entrees including ribs, crab cakes, and steak. Even though there is a big sports bar scene, the restaurants are family-friendly, and its signature feature is having a television at every table.

Silver Diner
www.silverdiner.com

With locations in Maryland, New Jersey, and Virginia, the Silver Diner is dedicated to bringing farm-fresh food to the table and has a great reputation in the community for buying local. The kids' menu has lots of choices, and there is even a gluten-free brownie sundae for dessert. The milkshakes here are to die for, and most locations have a weekly family night with entertainment from area children's performers, crafts or themed activities.

Spartans/Olympian's Family Restaurants
www.iloveolympians.com
www.ilovespartans.com

These family-owned sister restaurants (Spartan's in Burke and Olympians in Alexandria) feature classic casual fare and Greek specialties. The atmosphere is warm and friendly, and these restaurants continue to be local favorites. Spartan's is now open for breakfast on the weekends. Definitely try their delicious challah bread French toast! It is worth every calorie.

Best Places in the DC Metro Area to See or Ride Trains & Trolleys

B&O Railroad Museum
901 West Pratt Street
Baltimore, MD 21223
410-752-2490
www.borail.org

Burke Lake Park
7315 Ox Road
Fairfax Station, VA 22039
703-323-6600
www.fairfaxcounty.gov/parks/burkelakepark/rides.htm

Cabin John Regional Park
7400 Tuckerman Lane
Bethesda, MD 20817
301-299-0024
www.montgomeryparks.org

Dulles Town Center Express
21100 Dulles Town Circle
Sterling, VA 20166
703-421-4613
www.shopdullestowncenter.com/info/express

Fairfax Corner Express
4100 Monument Drive
Fairfax, VA 22030
703-222-4200
www.dudutrain.com

Fairfax Station Railroad Museum
11200 Fairfax Station Road
Fairfax Station, VA 22039
703-425-9225
www.fairfax-station.org

Manassas Historic Train Depot
9431 West Street
Manassas, VA 20110
703-368-1873
www.va-manassas2.civicplus.com

National Capital Trolley Museum
1313 Bonifant Road
Silver Spring, MD 20905
301-384-6088
www.dctrolley.org

National Zoo
3001 Connecticut Avenue Northwest
Washington, DC 20008
202-633-4888
www.nationalzoo.si.edu

Tysons Corner Center
1961 Chain Bridge Road
Tysons Corner, VA 22102
703-847-7300
www.shoptysons.com

Vienna Station & W&OD Caboose
231 Dominion Road NE
Vienna, VA 22180
703-255-6356
www.nvmr.org

Watkins Regional Park
301 Watkins Park Drive
Upper Marlboro, MD 20774
301- 218-6700
www.pgparks.com

Wheaton Regional Park
2000 Shorefield Road
Wheaton, MD 20902
301-905-3045
www.montgomeryparks.org

Best Stroller-Friendly Trails

Holmes Run Trail
Alexandria, VA
http://alexandriava.gov/recreation/

An 8 mile paved trail connecting different parks and nature centers in the City of Alexandria. See map at link for places to get on the trail.

Mount Vernon Trail
http://www.nps.gov/

18 mile paved multi-use trail (bikes and pedestrian) that connects the Mount Vernon Estate to Theodore Roosevelt Island. See trail map for parking places and attractions.

W & O Railroad Trail
http://www.nvrpa.org/park/w_od_railroad/

Built on the roadbed of the former Washington & Old Dominion Railroad, the W & O Trail offers 45 miles of paved trail from Shirlington in Arlington to the countryside of Purcellville in Loudoun.

Best Places for a Tea Party

American Girl Doll Store
8090L Tysons Corner Center
McLean, VA 22102
877-247-5223
www.americangirl.com

Carlyle House
121 N. Fairfax Street
Alexandria, VA 22314
703-549-2997
www.nvrpa.org/

Cherry Hill Farmhouse
312 Park Avenue
Falls Church, VA 22046
703 248-5171
www.fallschurchva.gov

Gadsby's Tavern
134 N. Royal Street
Alexandria, VA 22314
703-746-4242
www.alexandriava.gov/GadsbysTavern

Greenspring Gardens
4603 Green Spring Road
Alexandria, VA 22312
703-941-7987
www.fairfaxcounty.gov/parks/greenspring/teas.htm

Morrison House
116 South Alfred Street
Alexandria, VA 22314
703-838-8000
www.morrisonhouse.com

Oatlands Plantation
20850 Oatlands Plantation Lane
Leesburg, VA 20175
703.777.3174
www.oatlands.org

Pink Bicycle Tea Room
303 Commerce Street
Occoquan, VA 22125
703-491-5216
www.pinkbicycletearoom.com

Tea with Mrs. B
703 Lumsden Street
McLean, Virginia 22101
202-448-2930
www.teawithmrsb.com

Ritz-Carlton Tysons Corner
1700 Tysons Boulevard
McLean, VA 22102
703-506-4300
www.ritzcarlton.com

Woodlawn Plantation & Pope-Leighey House
9000 Richmond Highway
Mount Vernon, VA 22309
703-780-4000
http://www.woodlawn1805.org

About The Authors

About The Authors

Claudine Kurp

Claudine was motivated to start her first website DC Metro Mommy after the birth of her first daughter. Frustrated by the lack of local parenting resources for new mothers, she spent months curating a list of 4,000 vendors and created a guide and blog for local parents. After writing over 700 blogs and co-founding DC Metro Mom, a book was the next step in the journey to help families in the area. In a prior life, Claudine worked in Corporate America for 15 years. She often jokes that although there are similarities; executives are far easier to deal with than toddlers. She spends her time with her family and continues to discover new and wonderful things about the DC Metro area that she faithfully reports back to readers. She lives in Fairfax County, Virginia, with her two daughters and husband.

Amy Suski

Amy is mother to two sons, a daughter, and a rambunctious boxer dog. Before motherhood Amy worked in Washington, DC as an attorney and has since switched over to editing, blogging, and volunteering. She is co-founder of DC Metro Mom and loves to use her three children as guinea pigs to review plays, concerts, museums and other fun trips. She and her family have travelled across the USA, around Europe and the Caribbean. After living in Virginia for almost twenty years, she and her husband recently moved the family to the Boston area.

Micaela Williamson

Micaela is a travel-reading junkie and loves discovering books, brochures, and travel guides from all over the world. She can hardly contain her excitement for the Kid Trips project and loves scouting out different local venues with her family. A former elementary school teacher, Micaela's writing credentials include running a local parenting blog, being a mom blogger for the *Washington FAMILY Magazine*, and composing family feature articles for *Northern Virginia Magazine*. She resides with her husband and two young sons in Fairfax County, VA.

Connect With Us Online

Continue your Kid Trips journey by subscribing to our free blog and newsletter at www.GoKidTrips.com. If you found a broken link or error in this book please contact us at info@GoKidTrips.com. We appreciate and value your feedback.

Visit us at: http://www.GoKidTrips.com

Follow us on Facebook: www.facebook.com/GoKidTrips

Tweet with us on Twitter: www.twitter.com/GoKidTrips